Follow Me
Group Guide

This Is A Companion Guide To
Follow Me: The Disciple-making Strategy of Jesus

The book *Follow Me: The Disciple-making Strategy of Jesus*
may be ordered from
MasterWorks, Inc.
Dr. David E. Schroeder, Founder
info@masterworksinc.org

David E. Schroeder, Ed.D.

Copyright © 2013 by David E. Schroeder, Ed.D.

Follow Me Group Guide
The Disciple-making Strategy of Jesus
by David E. Schroeder, Ed.D.

Printed in the United States of America

ISBN 9781628394559

All rights reserved solely by the author. The author guarantees all contents are original and do not infringe upon the legal rights of any other person or work. No part of this book may be reproduced in any form without the permission of the author. The views expressed in this book are not necessarily those of the publisher.

Unless otherwise indicated, Bible quotations are taken from The HOLY BIBLE, NEW INTERNATIONAL VERSION®. NIV®. Copyright © 1973, 1978, 1984 by International Bible Society.

All other text in the Group Guide: Copyright © 1995 by MasterWorks, Inc. With the exception of the worksheet in the appendix, for which limited permission to photocopy is granted to owners of the manual, no materials may be copied without the permission of MasterWorks, Inc.

This is the sixth edition of the *"Follow Me" Group Guide* (formerly called *Manual*). It contains some material from earlier editions, but has been extensively rewritten based on experience in using the earlier versions. If, as you use this edition, you come up with suggestions that you think would improve it still further, please let us know.

Write to us at MasterWorks, Inc., info@masterworksinc.org. We would like to hear from you with any comments on how the materials have helped as well as any suggestions or problems.

Table of Contents

Introduction vii

Unit One: Learning Kingdom Values
Being a Disciple in Your Personal Life

Teachability 17
Flexibility 23
Humility 29
Compassion 34
Integrity 40

Unit Two: Learning Kingdom Ministry
Being a Disciple in the World

Selflessness 49
Intensity 55
Courage 62
Dependency 69
Transparency 75
Contentment 81

Unit Three: Learning Kingdom Leadership
Being a Disciple in the Church

Trustworthiness 91
Accountability 97
Alertness 103
Servanthood 109

Appendix 115

Introduction to the
"Follow Me" Group Guide

Perhaps the greatest challenge Jesus faced was not his impending death, but ensuring the life of the Christian church. No doubt he pondered it frequently. How could he in a short time communicate his spirit, his perspective on life, his lifestyle so deeply and fully to a small band of uneducated Galilean Jews that after his departure they would carry on his mission and message with such intensity and fervor that the whole world would be turned upside-down? (Acts 17:6)

History tells us he did it!—a social and political phenomenon without parallel. His impact on the disciples was so great that they bridged every barrier in the world with the gospel—culture, language, race, gender, generation, and terrain—so that for the past nineteen hundred years Christianity has been the dominant force on the earth.

Wouldn't it be great if we had a discipleship manual, authored by Jesus himself! Well, in a sense we do. The gospels are a succession of stories, events and teachings, many of them involving and focusing on the disciples. There is no doubt that, other than dying on the cross as the sacrifice for our sins, the highest priority of Jesus was training his disciples. To them he would commit the future of his church. They would play a strategic role in God's eternal plan of redemption.

So we should not be surprised to find ample material about what it means to be a disciple of Jesus Christ. In the book *"Follow Me"* and this Group Guide we focus mainly on those discipleship passages in Luke's Gospel. There we find fifteen recorded occasions where Jesus was specifically teaching one, three, twelve, or an unstated number of disciples. By extracting those passages from the rest of the narrative and general teaching, we have a rather authentic discipleship manual very close to the oral teaching of Jesus.

Disciples: On the Way

If you wanted to start a movement that would deeply affect all areas of the world and would be flourishing 2,000 years after you were gone, how would you do it? What kind of people would you select as your helpers?

Jesus chose a dozen people a lot like you—ordinary on the outside, but with hearts hungry to know and obey God. They were *not* people who were particularly religious as they (or we) would understand the term, but they were willing to pay a steep price to walk with God. And they "turned the world up-side down" in their day. Jesus Christ is still looking for people like that.

Some prefer an easier road in the Christian life, but if every Christian had followed the easy road, there would be no Christian church. Discipleship is the rough road of the kingdom of God, going against the traffic of the world.

It's a road strewn with obstacles, danger and mishaps, not a tour on a scenic cruiser designed to fill our leisure with luxury. It's the trailblazing of the pioneer. The Master didn't say, "Follow me, except when it's raining, snowing, hot or uphill." He didn't come to make life easy, but to make people spiritually strong. He came to make disciples.

But what is a disciple? How will I know if I am one, or becoming one? In a word, disciples of Jesus are people whose sole motivation is to be like their Master.

A disciple, when he is fully trained, will be like his teacher (Luke 6:40).

We need to be realistic. Jesus knew that the radical hate, the vicious crime, the fierce fighting, the gross injustice and the rampant ungodliness of our world and the human heart will not even begin to be challenged by a wimpish, faint-hearted, superficial Christianity. We need to know that same truth.

The world needs to see virile, committed disciples, not passive, lukewarm Christians. "Be like Jesus? A lofty and worthy goal," you might say, "but unattainable!" True. But should that put us off? What pitcher ever threw a two-hitter who wasn't trying for a no-hitter? What golfer ever hit a hole-in-one who was only trying to stay out of the rough? What pilot ever landed on the right runway at Logan Airport whose only goal was Boston? Becoming like Jesus is a lifelong pursuit. But don't despair. You don't become a disciple only when you've arrived; you are a disciple when you are earnestly on the way.

> On the way to gaining His WISDOM, that is. . .
>   Seeing life from God's point of view;
> On the way to accepting His LIFESTYLE, that is. . .
>   Living to express God's glory in every part of your life;
> On the way to developing His CHARACTER, that is. . .
>   Responding to all people and all situations selflessly;
> On the way to committing to His PRIORITIES, that is. . .
>   Seeking first the kingdom of God and His righteousness.

On The Way as a Disciple: A Development Project

When any builder begins a project, he must have in mind what the finished product will look like. Whether it's a skyscraper, a colonial style house or a bird house, he must have either a mental image, a sketch or precise blueprints of the end result. The same is true of our lives if we are successfully to attain spiritual goals. What should the finished product, a true disciple, be like? What is the pattern?

The finished product of discipleship is to be like the teacher, to be like Jesus. While we may like to know more about him, we already know more than we'll ever be able to use. The best earthly friend of Jesus, John the Apostle, tells us that by knowing Jesus we also know God the Father:

> *No man has ever seen God, but God the only Son, who is at the Father's side, has made him known* (John 1:18).

So as we become more like Jesus, we will become more godly.

What is godliness? In our work with scores of men in discipleship groups, we've noticed a sad but common phenomenon. Many fine Christian men are suffering unnecessarily from spiritual inferiority complexes. They are down on themselves, defeated. Not because they are trapped in sin, but simply because they fail to measure up to what they have been told is godliness, or deep spirituality.

A common thread seems to run through the fabric of these spiritual inferiority complexes. Most of these men have accepted a model of spirituality best described as *devotionalism*: a studious, quiet, reflective, contemplative spiritual life. Where have they gotten the idea that this is the pinnacle of discipleship? Not in the Bible! Most likely from the pulpits. Preachers, necessarily, must spend hours in quiet study and reflection, so that's the model they are most comfortable recommending. You meet God in the prayer closet or in your quiet time, they are fond of saying, as if God can't tolerate the dirt and the noise of the outside world.

Now this type of spirituality is wonderful. We admire those who use that approach to spiritual growth. Yet it is quite evident that Christianity wasn't put on the map by devotional types. At least as we define "devotional" today. The early Christians were devoted, true, but not to study and quiet time. They were devoted to a person, Jesus Christ their Lord. And he was an activist.

Gauging Godliness

How do we know that many of the early Christians didn't study or practice "quiet time" as we know these habits? Two facts. Many, if not most, of the early believers were illiterate. Slaves comprised a large part of the early church. For those few who could read, only the Old Testament, written in Hebrew, was available. It spoke primarily to the Jewish minority of the church, not to the vast majority of Gentiles. By the second century, B.C., some would have had access to the Septuagint, the Hebrew Bible translated into Greek. Secondly, even those who could read did not have ready access to the scriptures. This was true for centuries after Christ's life on earth. There were no family Bibles, pocket testaments, or personal study Bibles.

So these early Christians had to have a different standard of what constituted godliness. Certainly the teachings of Jesus handed down orally and later recorded by the Gospel writers were a major guide to godliness. Undoubtedly, Old Testament teaching became part of the formula, too. For example, David, who was an introspective individual, gave this very down-to-earth, socially involved depiction of the godly person:

> *Lord, who may dwell in your sanctuary?*
> *Who may live on your holy hill?*
> *He whose walk is blameless*
> *and who does what is righteous,*
> *who speaks the truth from his heart*
> *and has no slander on his tongue,*
> *who does his neighbor no wrong*
> *and casts no slur on his fellow man,*
> *who despises a vile man*
> *but honors those who fear the Lord,*
> *who keeps his oath*
> *even when it hurts,*
> *who lends his money without usury*

and does not accept a bribe against the innocent.
He who does these things will never be shaken. (Psalm 15)

There are many Christians who are living examples of Psalm 15, but because they're not devotional types they belittle their spirituality. Likewise, it concerns us how many we've known who do not do what is truly righteous—speak truth from the heart, etc.—but who feel smug in their spirituality because they abide by the quiet-time formula. Could it be that the standard of devotionalism as a gauge of godliness is a twentieth century expression of Pharisaism?

As we move through the discipleship passages of Luke's Gospel, we get a better understanding of what Francis Schaeffer calls, "true spirituality." Our remarks above are not intended to denigrate a devotional lifestyle. To be sure, we see Jesus withdrawing from the crowds for times of prayer. But if Jesus and the disciples had been only devotional, they would have died peacefully as good Jews. There would be no Christian church. It was as they took their spirituality into the world that their true righteousness confronted the corrupt religion and pagan state of their day. In the confrontation, God was able to speak and act.

HELP!!

There is no quick and easy formula to becoming a disciple of Jesus. Perhaps that's painfully obvious to you. So don't try to go it alone. You will need help. You will need the help of God's Holy Spirit giving you insight and power. You will need the help of God's holy Word giving you faith and direction. And you will need the help of God's holy community giving you encouragement and holding you accountable.

The people you are meeting with are all on the same road. To be sure, you are not in their shoes and they are not in yours, but you are all heading the same way. So help each other!

Help each other by caring for one another. Find out about the others' childhoods, their major turning points in life, their career dreams, their spiritual gifts, their sense of failure, their need for your help.

Help each other by challenging one another. Become a team, so that no one wins unless you all win. Challenge each other to grow in godliness. To do this you will have to develop trusting relationships. Only then can you shed the macho mask or cosmetic cover that keeps us all from becoming truly mature men and women. Discipleship is best learned in a group setting. For example, the incident in which James and John were jockeying for preferential treatment in the kingdom aroused the ire of the other ten. This gave Jesus an opportunity to admonish all of them about servant-leadership. (See Mark 10:35-45.)

We also recommend that your group be men only. Experience has taught convincingly that most people do not become spiritually intimate (open, transparent, vulnerable) in a mixed group. Nor should they, in our opinion, except in the husband/wife relationship. Furthermore, men are challenged spiritually in many areas where they need other male input, but these topics may not easily be addressed in mixed groups. The same is true of women.

Growth in Groups

This workbook is intended to be used in conjunction with *"Follow Me"*, authored by David E. Schroeder. The Group Guide is written in such a manner that you can use it by itself. If you use the text and Guide together, we recommend that you read the pertinent chapter individually and then use the workbook in the group meetings.

Ideally there should be five to eight members in your group, small enough to develop spiritual intimacy, yet large enough to benefit from a variety of gifts and experiences.

Our goal in preparing this workbook has been to write conversationally, as if we were meeting with you. We've tried to introduce each discussion session with a few paragraphs that reflect on one of the discipleship passages from Luke. We recommend that you read these paragraphs out loud. Doing so insures that you are all beginning at the same place; it also serves to focus the group and reduce the likelihood of rambling. Following the groups of paragraphs, there are several questions designed to help you reflect on the topic and apply it to your life, your relationships and responsibilities. The questions are not meant to be threatening or complex; they are designed to help you see the degree to which each discipleship quality is (or can become) part of your life.

Your goal is not to complete the lessons, but to grow spiritually. Keep reminding yourselves to focus on the maturity, not on the material in the Guide. Jesus himself took at least three years with his twelve disciples, and he was with them day and night over that time. Expect to see growth, but don't demand it overnight.

A Typical Discipleship Meeting

There is no one right way to hold these meetings. Nevertheless, we know that not everybody is comfortable planning a small group meeting totally on their own. You may be one of those people. So the suggestions that follow are meant to help you become more confident. Our experience has led us to trust that if you get the right people together, sharing the goal of growing as disciples, the scripture verse will be fulfilled: *For where two or three come together in my name, there am I with them* (Matthew: 18:20).

When/Where You can meet any time of day or night, whenever is most convenient for the members of the group. Meet any place, public or private, where the people can concentrate. The same place, same hour each week has benefits, but going to one another's homes can be helpful. Most common meeting times:

- a regular weekly breakfast in a coffee shop or in the homes of the members;
- lunch time at work
- early Saturday morning
- Sunday School hour at church
- Commuters could meet on the train

Frequency We strongly recommend meeting weekly; less frequently than that will seriously hinder progress.

Every two weeks is okay, though it requires discipline to stick with it at the start, and it will take much longer to become comfortable enough with each other to share deeply.

Structure We recommend the following as a general routine:

1. Scripture reading
Have one member read the passage from Luke on which the lesson is based. Since you will use the same passage for several weeks in a row, you may want to vary the translations in succeeding weeks.

2. Opening prayer, to gain awareness of Christ's presence
Brief: there will be more time later.

3. Follow up open items - 3-5 minutes
Review key points, experiences, applications, and learnings since the last session.

4. Guide - 30-45 minutes
The section below on the use of this Guide gives some general guidelines for this part of the meeting.

5. Prayer - 15-25 minutes
Spend time praying specifically with and for one another. Have one member be the prayer coordinator, keeping a list of requests. Some weeks you may wish to begin the meeting with the prayer session.

Overall duration 60-90 minutes

This Guide If you use *"Follow Me" Group Guide* in conjunction with *"Follow Me"* encourage the people in your group to read the textbook on their own. As each character quality section of the Guide will (typically) take three or more weeks to complete, they will have ample time to read the corresponding chapters in the textbook.

You will notice that there are four sections in each chapter:

- *What It Says* takes you into the biblical text with a brief comment on the historical context. You might ask someone to read that aloud at the beginning of your first meeting on the chapter.
- *What It Means* consists of three lessons that focus mostly on understanding what the disciples understood Jesus to be saying and how that was likely to impact them.
- *What It Means for Me* leads the group into application of the text to daily living, and is intended to help group members share their spiritual lives with each other.
- *Now What?* will take individuals or the group into ideas for further study, reflection, or action.

Try not to focus too much on the content, looking for right and wrong answers. The material is not an end in itself. It is but a means toward the end. The end is producing godly disciples who live much as the Master did, even if they never become wordsmiths, able to articulate the essence of each of the fifteen qualities.

Leadership Consider your meetings to be times of learning, but don't conduct them as classroom experiences. Try to have one member who is able to act as facilitator, not as a lecturer. Such a leader is not a teacher, but a guide.

In an appendix to this manual, there is a section giving more specific leadership suggestions. Turn there for more detailed guidelines, or if you experience problems.

Freedom Each member should strive to come to each meeting prepared. Most will want to fill in the blanks of the Guide. Don't, however, become slavish to the Guide. Skip questions that may not be profitable. Don't put anyone on the spot by pushing for answers. And don't make the mistake of thinking that the ones who perform academically are necessarily more advanced spiritually.

Even though we hope the Group Guide will be helpful in your meetings, you should feel free to depart totally from it in any given session. For example, you may sense that more growth can take place or is needed through following up on a life experience being shared by one of the members. Or you may want to help one another talk through a problem. It's more important to complete the individual than to complete the material.

Assessing your progress against the 15 Discipleship Qualities

You are going to be working through passages in Luke in which Jesus directly addressed the twelve, and sometimes others who were following him closely. In these passages we have identified fifteen character qualities that Jesus was seeking to develop in those who would follow him.

In the appendix to this workbook, you'll find each of those qualities listed on a worksheet. This worksheet has proved to be useful to some who have worked through this material before you. Each quality appears on a continuum. We encourage you to take a copy of this sheet and give it to family members, friends, coworkers, any people who know you well. Ask them to place a mark on each scale at the point that describes you. You may want to do this several times during the course of the months that you are studying this material. As we said above, however, don't expect to move immediately to the "ideal" end of each scale. But do listen to the feedback of those who love you.

Becoming a Disciple-maker

While none of us will ever achieve perfection as a disciple of Jesus, he wants us – and has commanded us – to make disciples of others. That is the true purpose of the *"Follow Me" Group Guide* – to provide for you material and a strategy for making disciples of others. "So, "you may ask," what are the qualifications and definition of a disciple-maker?" We see it as:

Disciple-making is modeling, teaching and motivating others to be like Jesus. It is "reprogramming" their worldview and lifestyle from the errors of this culture (including religion) to the culture of God's kingdom.

Before launching into the lessons, please receive this word of encouragement. We believe God is very pleased when his sons and daughters take seriously his goal for them to become like his Son, Jesus

Christ. We also believe that he has created you for good works. The verse behind the name of our group, MasterWorks, is Ephesians 2:10: *We are his workmanship, created in Christ Jesus for good works*. Some of those good works include making disciples of others, and you can or will be able to do it. Here is the Word of encouragement in John 15:16, Jesus said to his first followers:

You did not choose me, but I chose you and appointed you so that you might go and bear fruit – fruit that will last – and so that whatever you ask in my name the Father will give you.

UNIT ONE

LEARNING KINGDOM VALUES
Being a Disciple in Your Personal Life

- Teachability
- Flexibility
- Humility
- Compassion
- Integrity

CHAPTER ONE

OBEYING ANYHOW

Disciple Quality: **TEACHABILITY**

WHAT IT SAYS

LESSON ONE
Read LUKE 5:1-11

The calling of the four fishermen, Peter, Andrew, James, and John, was a turning point in the ministry of Jesus. Certainly he could have continued doing miracles and presenting his marvelous teaching without anyone's help, and certainly he could have gone to the cross without having any disciples, but he chose not to. Why?

The question becomes even more compelling when we consider the gospel accounts, which show the twelve disciples to be excess baggage to the ministry of Jesus. They were slow to learn, short of faith, selfishly ambitious, and insensitive to the purposes and methods of Jesus. They did nothing to enhance his image or reputation. When the chips were down and Jesus was arrested, they abandoned him. So why did Jesus bother with these fishermen or any other disciples?

> *The disciples were slow to learn, short of faith, selfishly ambitious, and insensitive to the purposes and methods of Jesus.*

The answer does not appear until we get to Luke's second volume, the *Acts of the Apostles*. After they were empowered at Pentecost, the disciples were radically transformed into dynamic, fearless, faith-full, world-changing men. Many people marvel at the power of Pentecost as though it alone explains the subsequent success of the apostles. It does not. There were 120 who had the same experience, but most of them passed into history anonymously.

Pentecost was the fuel of the early church. The machinery that propelled the earliest disciples was the three years of kingdom training Jesus gave. When the Holy Spirit filled them, what was their message; what was their method? Did they develop a new theology and a new strategy? Not according to scripture. We find that they continued preaching the kingdom of God and showing the power of that kingdom in the same ways Jesus did. In other words, they were able to continue the ministry of Jesus because they had been teachable. And that is why he called them to be with him. Yes, he cared about their individual conversion, but making disciples was just as important. Conversion results in the spiritual birth of individuals; making disciples resulted in the birth of the church.

What was it that caused them to take this risk? Did they understand what they were getting into? Did they know what it meant to "catch men"? Undoubtedly they knew or understood very little. What drew them was the powerful spiritual magnetism of Jesus. His personal righteousness, his penetrating insight into the ways of God, his perception of their own character, his power over nature, and most impressively, the presence of God in his life drew these men to fulfill a destiny in which they would become the pillars of the church. Perhaps they had a choice about following him, but any other kind of life would be stale and meaningless in comparison.

As you consider your relationship to Jesus, you may wonder whether he recruited you to follow him or whether you made the decision to be "saved" to avoid going to hell. Or maybe you are not sure whether you are a follower or whether you're saved. Wherever you are in relation to Jesus, you can be sure he knows you and invites you to follow him. Your **teachability** will determine how well you follow him.

In the scripture lesson that introduces our study of Jesus and his disciples, we find Simon Peter at work, on the job. In fact, Peter has had a hard day "at the office." He'd been out all night and had nothing to show for it. (No "net" profit!) And here comes a traveling preacher who borrows his boat for a short time of teaching, interrupting the necessary task of cleaning and repairing the nets. Luke doesn't tell us what Jesus said on that day. We may presume it was something like his teachings recorded in Luke 6:20-48, or perhaps like the "Sermon on the Mount" as recorded in Matthew 5-7. In any event, having already extended Peter's workday, this Jesus has the gall to tell Peter to go back to work!

1. Had Peter chosen not to obey Jesus' command to go out fishing again, what excuses might he have made? (See the section under "Unpleasant, Humiliating, Unreasonable" in Chapter One of *"Follow Me"*.)

2. Why was Peter so moved by the large catch?

    What did he recognize about Jesus? About himself?

3. What difference did it make that Jesus first helped Peter and friends succeed in their job when things weren't going well before asking them to give up fishing?

4. Notice that Peter did not ask Jesus to go into the fishing business with him rather than going into business with Jesus. How do we sometimes try to drag Jesus into "doing our thing"?

5. How do you think Peter understood the "catching men" remark?

    Is this an activity Jesus wants us to do? If so, how can we be prepared to do it?

WHAT IT MEANS

LESSON TWO

Notice how Jesus established rapport with the four fishermen (see parallel passages Mark 1:16-20 and Matthew 4:18-22 for the calling of all four). He did not send for them to come to Nazareth where he might impress them with his carpentry skills. No, he went to them, to their profession, and used it to build rapport. Using his supernatural ability (power over nature), he quickly demonstrated that life can be more than seeing how many fish one can net. The abundant catch of fish also convinced them of his ability to provide for them if they were to follow him.

> *By leaving everything to go with him, they were exposing themselves and their families to material devastation.*

6. What is your most unpleasant, routine task?

    What might it be teaching you about being a disciple of Jesus?

7. What was one unreasonable expectation of you made by your boss or other authority figure?

    What was your response? Did you demonstrate the quality of **teachability**?

8. What difficult demand from the Lord have you obeyed?

    How did obeying contribute to your growth?

9. How can obedience to unpleasant, routine or unreasonable tasks help us learn how to handle success?

    Why is **teachability** such an important kingdom value for a disciple?

WHAT IT MEANS FOR ME

LESSON THREE

From Old Testament prophets we learn that God is not pleased with people who are arrogant and "stiff-necked," insisting on going their own way. **Teachability**—a willingness to listen, to heed, and to obey—is what he seeks. **Teachability** is not necessarily found in the highly educated. It is not the ability to grasp intricate details, to retain volumes of information; in short, it is not a matter of intelligence. It is a matter of the will.

Pride is probably the predominant underlying obstacle to **teachability**. Pride keeps me closed to the possibility that another person has something to say which might legitimately challenge my established ways of doing things. Pride is what keeps me smug with myself as I am, unwilling to pay any respectful attention to another point of view.

10. Focus on Jesus' words, *"Put out into deep water, and let down the nets for a catch."* If Jesus were to speak these words into your life right now, what would he likely be asking you to do? How might it involve a step of faith?

11. If "no fish" = little success, "many fish" = human success, and "men" = spiritual success, in terms of your career, ministry and personal growth what phrase best expresses your situation? (Circle one for each line.)

Career:	no fish	many fish	men
Ministry:	no fish	many fish	men
Personal growth:	no fish	many fish	men

12. In Matthew 13:1-23 Jesus told about three obstacles to **teachability** as three kinds of unproductive soil:

- Hardened soil = prejudices
- Rocky soil = preferences
- Thorny soil = preoccupations

Which is the greatest threat to your **teachability**? You may wish to review the sections after "Soil Analysis" in Chapter One of *"Follow Me"*.

13. Under what circumstances does your heart's soil become more fertile—softer, deeper, cleaner?

What can be done to cultivate the seed of the Word planted in you?

14. In calling us to obedience Jesus often demands that we forsake our natural inclinations. What are our natural inclinations, and what are God's principles in the following areas?

Topic	Natural Inclinations	God's Principles (References)
Financial Gain		Luke 12:32-34
Popularity		Luke 6:26-28
Getting even		Rom 12:17, 21
Success		Matt 16:25
Leadership		Matt 20:26-27
Respect		Luke 14:1-14
Pleasure		Psalm 37:4
Independence		Rom 13:1-2
Joy		James 1:2-3

15. This question may take a few weeks to complete. To get to know one another better, each person should tell his or her story, and specifically answer: "When did you first hear Jesus say to you, 'Follow Me'?"

Pray with one another to grow in the quality of **teachability**, learning to obey Jesus.

NOW WHAT?

Kingdom Strategy #1

Disciples of Jesus Christ must be readily teachable, even to the point of obeying seemingly absurd commands that violate our natural inclinations.

What was it that Jesus saw in Peter that made him a candidate for recruitment? Physical charisma? Superior intelligence? Potential leadership? Flamboyant personality? All of these were part of the fisherman, but none of them endeared him to Jesus. It was one quality: **TEACHABILITY**, the willingness, even the eagerness to embrace new truths though they may dismantle natural inclinations and prejudices. Peter's aptitude as a student would be tested time and time again. He often failed the impromptu quizzes of life but not for lack of **teachability**.

Teachability is the most basic quality of any disciple. The word *disciple* literally means "learner," and is descriptive of people who are open to new input, not just on the theoretical level but on the practical plane of daily living. In other words, teachable people are not hostile toward change.

Many people are good students in that they will eagerly absorb new facts and ideas that appeal to their minds. Fewer are good disciples, who also embrace new truth that tampers with their will. It's one thing to expand my pool of knowledge; it's another thing to meddle with my motivations and lifestyle!

Teachability is not a property like freckles which you either have or do not have. Rather, **teachability** is a quality which you may cultivate, as Peter did. Using the texts listed below, trace Peter's spiritual growth in **teachability**.

Text	Peter's Response
John 1:40-42	
Luke 5:1-11	
Matt. 14:28-33	
Matt. 16:13-19	
Matt. 16:21-23	
Matt. 17:1-8	
Matt. 18:21-22	
Matt. 26:69-75	
John 13:6-10	
John 18:10-11	
John 20:1-8	
John 21:15-23	

You may wish to continue this study in the *Book of Acts* to see how Peter's **teachability** continued to grow. Now, do one or both of the following personal exercises:

a. Reflecting on your life thus far, record in a journal the significant events that gave you opportunity to grow in **teachability**.

b. Begin a journal with a "**Teachability**" section, and record daily or at least weekly which experiences you believe God is using in your life to build your **teachability** quotient.

CHAPTER TWO

WELCOMING NEWNESS

Disciple Quality: **FLEXIBILITY**

WHAT IT SAYS

LESSON FOUR
Read Luke 5:27-39

Reaching out to social outcasts seems to have been a ministry that particularly delighted Jesus. In the first few chapters of Luke we see Jesus touching the lives of demonized people, a leper, a paralytic, and tax collectors, the most despised of all outcasts. The contrast between them and the Pharisees could not have been more stark. Tax collectors were likely the least religious of all Jews.

Calling lower class fishermen to follow him was tolerable, even if a bit unusual, but by recruiting a tax collector, Jesus convinced the Pharisees that he really was out of step with orthodox Judaism. They must have been shocked to find him eating with tax collectors and other sinners at Levi's reception—a daring thing for Jesus to do, but thoroughly consistent with his mission.

> *Calling lower class fishermen to follow him was tolerable, even if a bit unusual, but by recruiting a tax collector...*

We see **FLEXIBILITY** as the key discipleship quality here because those who follow Jesus must be willing to reject the rigid religions that are based on human performance, and they must whole-heartedly embrace an explosive, dynamic, fermenting kingdom. Disciples cannot be people who shun change. Indeed, they must adopt a lifestyle of repentance—*metanoia*—which means to change your mind and your behavior.

1. How do the images of garments and wineskins illustrate the point Jesus was making about **flexibility**?

    Is **flexibility** the same as uncritical tolerance?

2. Biblical terms that express the idea of **flexibility** are "forbearance" and "tolerance."

    What do the following verses say about these concepts?

    Romans 2:4

    Ephesians 4:2

    Colossians 3:13

3. Whom in scripture, history, or your experience do you admire for his/her **flexibility**?

    Can you share a story that will illustrate this?

4. As in the parables of the patches and wine, how is Christianity sometimes

    Shrunken down?

    Added onto?

    Contained and shaped?

5. With respect to changing, what is the difference between **flexibility** and fickleness?

WHAT IT MEANS

LESSON FIVE

Luke 5:34-37 certainly made for some interesting table talk. Quite likely, the reference to the bride and the bridegroom reminded the Pharisees of the three passages in Jeremiah (7:34, 16:9, 25:10), which predicted the removal of celebrations of bridegrooms and brides during the Babylonian captivity. The prophecy also speaks about the restoration of *"the voice of the bridegroom and the voice of the bride"* (33:11) once the exiles have returned. This was a pointed way for Jesus to say that Pharisaism was a religion of captivity, whereas his people were disciples of freedom and restoration.

The bondage of Pharisaic Judaism was a denial of the kingdom of God; they were still in exile, not in the land of the Lord of liberation. Verse 35 doubtlessly refers to the time of grief the disciples would experience for three days while Jesus was dead. The word for "taken away" suggests a violent removal by death. The joy of his resurrection and abiding presence in the person of the Holy Spirit, however, keep his people, the guests of the bridegroom, rejoicing and celebrating. Gloom and doom religion is not Christianity.

In the other two parables the operative word is "new," which occurs eight times in the four verses. The incongruity of the new patch to the old garment and the new wine to the old wineskin shows how Jesus viewed the relationship between his kingdom and Pharisaic Judaism. The two could not possibly mix; certainly the kingdom could not be sewn onto or contained by Judaism. New garments and new wineskins are important for the fabric and fermentation of a new kingdom!

> *New garments for the fabric and new wineskins for the fermentation of a new kingdom!*

At first the Pharisees complained to Jesus' disciples about his eating and drinking with such rabble, but after Jesus silenced them by saying that this was his mission (vv. 31, 32), they retreated to the issue of merely eating and drinking. If they couldn't disarm him on the issue of the company he kept, they would attack his lack of dietary piety. Implied in their condemnation was the superiority of their disciples and even those of John the Baptist over the disciples of Jesus.

6. What might Jesus do today that would offend the religious establishment?

7. What might he do that would upset your spiritual or religious sensitivities?

8. Do you agree that it is difficult for religious people to be flexible? Why?

9. What are some hindrances to **flexibility**?

10. Why is **flexibility** such an extremely important *kingdom* value? How can established churches keep from becoming fossilized?

11. What new wineskins may be needed today for the gospel of the kingdom?

WHAT IT MEANS FOR ME

LESSON SIX

People who work in cross-cultural situations, like missionaries, realize that without **flexibility**, they will have no ministry. But "cross-cultural" doesn't mean just crossing and ocean; it may mean "across the kitchen table." Raising teenagers, especially, requires godly **flexibility**. Every generation finds a way to offend the older generation—whether it be in clothes, music, activities, hair styles, whatever. Parents can get hung up on these external symbols and become judgmental, thus destroying the relationship. Can you imagine going to China on a missions trip and saying to the Chinese, "I hate your food; you wear funny clothes; and you have weird customs," and then expect them to learn to love your Jesus?

In singling out **flexibility** as a primary quality of discipleship, we are not implying that every change ought to be welcomed or even tolerated. Sometimes changes are wrong; other times it is wrong not to change. The principle of **flexibility** calls for the willingness to consider changing, and the ability to welcome newness when it is best for God's work.

12. One pastor responded to a thorny question during a candidating interview by distinguishing between absolutes, convictions, opinions, and prejudices. Using his categories, how willing do you think we should be to consider change in these areas?

	Welcome It	Tolerate It	Resist It
Absolutes			
Convictions			
Opinions			
Prejudices			

13. What are some of the old garments and old wineskins of Christianity?

    How have these affected your growth?

14. Take a clear-eyed look at yourself. Think about what others, especially those close to you, may have said about your attitude toward change. Then mark the scales below to indicate your tendencies. Try to think about how you may act differently depending on the setting.

	Usually I insist on doing things in the established way. Change happens "over my dead body!"	I'm willing to listen to advocates of change. Sometimes I even agree to it	I initiate change. Frequently I experiment with new ways of doing things.
At work, with co-workers			
At home, with my family			
In church, with fellow members			
In the community, with neighbors			

15. Having looked at those general areas of your life, have you have been inflexible and rigid lately towards:

    ____ A person?

    ____ A new method or idea?

    ____ A new plan?

    ____ Someone else's scruples, or lack of?

16. What are some of the underlying reasons you become rigid?

17. What are some principles that might help parents walk the fine line between being uncritically tolerant and being flexible?

18. Based on these lessons, with respect to change, do you consider yourself to be:

    ____ Rigid   ____ Laid back   ____ Skeptical

    ____ Eager   ____ Hesitant   ____ Flexible

Looking back at question 18, do you need to make some changes? Why not ask one or all of the people in your group to pray with you about growing in **flexibility** and then plan to report back next week?

NOW WHAT?

Kingdom Strategy #2

Citizenship in the kingdom of God must be seen as an entirely new and unique life calling, not as something to be added to the old life.

This lesson uses the imagery of wineskins and wine. Because wine speaks of life, vitality, transformation, it is often a symbol of the Holy Spirit in Scripture. What is Jesus saying here? Simply this—what you are receiving when you receive the kingdom is so new and dynamic that none of your old receptacles, none of your old structures and forms, are able to contain it.

Wineskins, of course, are made of leather, and new leather is very flexible. Old leather is rigid and cracks easily. Jesus was saying that the kingdom is always in fermentation. In grape juice or other organic material, fermentation is a chemical reaction that causes expansion, which is why the cork on a wine bottle pops when the bottle is opened. If unfermented or "new" wine is poured into an old, rigid, inflexible wineskin and then ferments, there will be an explosion. Fermentation demands **flexibility** or "soft skins."

Jesus was teaching here that people who want the new wine of the kingdom of God must be flexible. Kingdom life is too dynamic to be contained by rigid skins that it cannot shape. God's kingdom will not settle into the shape of any earthly mold. The absolutely essential quality we need for this new life-changing gift is **flexibility**. Because church structures and dogmas can be quite rigid, it is often difficult for religious people to change. But Jesus said that if you are going to be a kingdom person, you must not expect to be able to use the "old wineskins" of your former life.

Flexibility is one of the kingdom qualities especially needed for our life in the our life in the our life in the church. The challenge to be flexible was given by Jesus to religious people. Ralph Neighbour has written a book titled *The Seven Last Words of the Church*[i], subtitled "We've Never Done It That Way Before." Usually those words are said with a tinge of pride and a dose of stubbornness, implying, "And we're not about to start changing now!" It may be illuminating and helpful for you or your group to anticipate how you'd respond to changes in the following areas of church life: (Put an X in one column next to each phrase.) Compare answers and discuss your reasons.

	Welcome It	Tolerate It	Resist It
Other ethnic people			
A different order of worship			
"Seeker sensitive" services			
Longer sermons			
Shorter sermons			
A building project			
Women on the church board			
Starting a Christian school			
Contemporary music			
Hymns only			
More missionary emphasis			
Inter-church cooperation			
Social activism			
Use of liturgy			
Dress-down mode			
Drama			

CHAPTER THREE

REJOICING IN ADVERSITY

Disciple Quality: **HUMILITY**

WHAT IT SAYS

LESSON SEVEN
Read Luke 6:20-26

In Luke 6:23, Jesus tells his disciples to *Rejoice in that day and leap for joy.* Americans often see people leaping for joy—the Super Bowl victors, the big prize winner on a game show, the homecoming of a hostage, an election victory. But Jesus speaks of rejoicing because of the blessings of poverty, hunger, tears, and rejection.

Blessings? Our world considers wealth, abundance, laughter, and applause to be blessings, not their opposites. Are Christians to be so odd that they experience life opposite to normal human emotions and responses? Are we to be masochists or have martyr complexes?

We come now to a teaching that really goes contrary to conventional thinking. It is simply not natural to rejoice in adversity. People in the world respect, though not always practice, the two preceding discipleship qualities—teachability and flexibility. But here, in the "Sermon on the Plain," Jesus takes some of the very goals that most people seek—wealth, luxury, happiness and fame—and proclaims "Woe" to those who seek them, while those who do not aspire to those goals are called "Blessed."

> *Jesus takes some of the very goals that most people seek—wealth, luxury, happiness and fame—and proclaims "Woe"*

This passage needs careful study and interpretation. Notice that Jesus said, *"Blessed are you who are. . . ."* He may not have been recommending that lifestyle for everyone, but he surely wanted his followers who already were experiencing poverty, hunger, etc., to know that those negative realities could well be a source of blessing. Likewise, the rich, well fed, happy, and popular are warned that those realities do not imply blessing.

The force of the teaching is that one's situation in life, whether pleasant or not, is not necessarily the indication of God's blessing. In fact, since wealth, health, and happiness often promote an independent, self-sufficient attitude, less fortunate people have greater possibility to be truly blessed because of their reliance upon God.

Humility is the character quality being emphasized here. It's a tough one to tackle, but a most important one. Let's begin with a long, hard, honest look at ourselves. Although honesty is not the quality we are considering here, it really underlies **humility**. Francis Frangipane, in *Holiness, Truth and the Presence of God*[ii], observes that holiness begins when we honestly recognize the enormity of God and the relative smallness of man. It is true that God has bestowed some dignity upon us by creating us in his own image, but the distance between the being of God and *homo sapiens* is far greater than the distance between an ant and a man. In light of a God who created and controls a universe of over 100 billion galaxies, **humility** ought to come rather easily to human beings. For some strange reason, it does not.

One reason we cannot approach holiness in our lives without **humility** is that holiness is a byproduct of grace, not of works, and as James 4:6 says, *God gives grace to the humble*.

1. State the main lesson Jesus taught in Luke 6:20-26.

2. In their context, what might the disciples have thought about:

    - Poverty

    - Hunger

    - Sorrow/sadness

    - Rejection

3. What do the "woes" in Luke 6:24-26 imply?

4. Is it wrong to try to be happy?

    If not, how do you reconcile that with verses 24-26?

    Is it possible to pursue happiness too zealously?

WHAT IT MEANS

LESSON EIGHT

Underlying all the Beatitudes is the kingdom quality of **humility**. If we crave ever-greater financial and social status, letting materialistic success symbols become obsessions to us, we will be of little value to the work of God's kingdom and poor representatives of what the kingdom is all about. While poverty, hunger, weeping, and rejection may not be part of our life goals, neither should obtaining wealth, feasting lavishly, living as though life is always a party, and seeking popularity.

A big part of **humility** is contentment: rejoicing in adversity. People of the kingdom are not self-strivers; they are not out to elevate their own status according to the values of the world. This is not to say that the poor and hungry should be happy *about* their poverty and starving. Rather, disciples are to be content with the lowly status and reputation usually reserved for the poor and hungry. Social climbing is contrary to kingdom living. The only worthy elevation in the kingdom is on the cross.

5. Describe the **humility** that you believe a disciple of Jesus should manifest.

    Why is **humility** such an important value of the kingdom of God?

6. Have you ever experienced a time of poverty, hunger, weeping, or rejection and you sensed it was a blessing?

    If so, tell about it.

    If not, looking back on such an experience, can you now see any blessing that came from it?

7. In what ways have you experienced rejection?

    Why is rejection humiliating?

    Paul, in Philippians 4:11-12, demonstrates the quality of **humility**: *I am not saying this because I am in need, for I have learned to be content whatever the circumstances. I know what it is to be in need, and I know what it is to have plenty. I have learned the secret of being content in any and every situation, whether well fed or hungry, whether living in plenty or in want.*

8. What experience do you think helped Paul learn the contentment he claims?

9. Can you recount experiences that have helped you learn to be content?

10. Are humble people likely to be respected?

    If not, why not?

    If need be, which should one sacrifice first: respect or **humility**? Why?

WHAT IT MEANS FOR ME

LESSON NINE

For the follower of Jesus Christ to be able to rejoice during the humiliation of poverty, hunger, weeping, and rejection, he must dance to a different drumbeat than intrigues the rest of the world. The Apostle Paul knew well that different drumbeat since he knew well the drummer. In Philippians 2:3-8 Paul exhorts his fellow disciples,

> *Your attitude should be the same as that of Christ Jesus:*
> *Who, being in the very nature of God*
> *did not consider equality with God*
> *something to be grasped,*
> *but made himself nothing,*
> *taking the very nature of a servant,*
> *being made in human likeness.*
> *And being found in appearance as a man,*
> *he humbled himself*
> *and became obedient to death—*
> *even death on a cross!*

Paul knew that Jesus Christ had not only paid the price on the cross for mankind's salvation, but had also shown the perfect pattern for living. Jesus was always poor, he may often have been hungry, and he surely experienced plenty of sorrow and rejection. Yet, because of his intimate life with God, Jesus was blessed. Paul wanted more than anything else to emulate Christ's life, even by suffering (see Philippians 3:10). That pattern of life still stands as the model for all of Christ's followers: humble obedience as a servant of God.

Christians can rejoice when poverty, hunger, and tears help to etch indelibly in their redeemed lives the pattern of Christ's life. Christians should leap for joy when Christ's life shines so brightly in their lives that they are rejected by those estranged from God and choosing to live in darkness. By God's grace, the discomfort that first forces rejection may later kindle in the lost children of God a yearning to come home.

11. How does a Christian learn to be humble?

    Can a humble person know he or she is humble?

    Is **humility** primarily action or attitude?

12. In what aspect of your life do you have the most difficult time being humble?

13. What kinds of things can we do to achieve genuine **humility**?

Earlier in the *"Follow Me" Group Guide*, we looked at teachability as an important character quality. Teachability was described as obedience, an obedience that is willing to forsake natural inclinations, willing to obey even when obedience might appear foolish. Ponder the connections between **humility** and obedience in Philippians 2:8. While being humble may precede acts of obedience, it is also true that obeying God by doing acts of service for others can help one learn **humility**.

14. What might it mean for you, now, following Christ's example, to **humble** yourself?

    What specific areas of obedience are blocked in your life by an unwillingness or inability to humble yourself?

15. What might it mean for you, now, to follow Christ's example and become *"obedient unto death"*?

NOW WHAT?

Kingdom Strategy #3

Disciples of Jesus accept and live by an economic, social, and moral value system that is contrary to the world and to natural human inclinations.

Andrew Murray ends his book, *Humility*[iii], with this paragraph:

May God teach us to believe that to be humble, to be nothing in His presence, is the highest attainment and the fullest blessing of the Christian life. He speaks to us: "I dwell in the high and holy place, and with him that is of a contrite and humble spirit" (Isaiah 57:15). Be this our destiny!

In contrast, a tee shirt in Palo Alto, California, bore the pronouncement: "Oh God, it's so hard to be humble when you're from Stanford."

Return to question 12 in Lesson Nine. Share your "Stanford" with at least one other member of your group; that is, openly discuss the area of life in which each of you has the most difficulty being biblically humble. Make a commitment to work at attaining a Christlike perspective, and ask your fellow disciples to hold you accountable for making progress.

Ponder deeply the implications of 1 Peter 5:6:

Humble yourselves, therefore, under God's mighty hand, that he may lift you up in due time.

CHAPTER FOUR

RESPONDING TO REJECTION

Disciple Quality: **COMPASSION**

WHAT IT SAYS

LESSON TEN
Read Luke 6:27-38

Peering into the future of his disciples' lives, Jesus could see some storm clouds gathering. He knew that they would face much conflict and rejection. He also knew that being rejected would give them opportunities to show the difference between natural responses and kingdom responses. The natural response to hostility is either to run or to fight; in other words to react negatively to an "enemy." Kingdom living calls for a positive, compassionate commitment to those who reject you. This would be an expensive lesson for the disciples to learn. Some of them, including Jesus himself, would pay for the principle with their lives.

The key to modeling this radical life effectively is not for a few individuals to respond obediently, for it is easy for skeptics to explain away isolated extremism. But when a whole body of people, who in every other way are "sane," is seen to be compassionate, others will be encouraged to obey Jesus also. This principle has potential to shake up the community, the state, the nation, and the world. Whenever the kingdom of God is acting in power, the Spirit of God is renewing the church, and evangelism is going forward dynamically, it is because we Christians are taking these teachings very seriously. Jesus blesses obedience, not excuses.

This world is no friend of grace, nor is it a friend of righteousness. From the human point of view, our Lord's crucifixion was plotted by the religious leaders for one reason: they could not tolerate the gaze of his pure eyes. If the Lord's disciples are to live by the pattern which he gave in the Beatitudes, surely they also will arouse the wrath of people in the world who live for a different kingdom.

The passage we are looking at now, Luke 6:27-38, is preceded by Luke's version of the Beatitudes. It is because such a lifestyle confronts our fallen nature that Jesus expects his followers to have enemies, haters, cursers, and mistreaters. Knowing that they would be rejected for the sake of righteousness, Jesus wanted to warn his disciples and instruct them how to respond.

But more than warning them, Jesus wanted to tell them how to respond to rejection. The natural human responses to rejection are retaliation or retreat, neither of which is a kingdom response. Perhaps the example of Jesus should have been enough, for he consistently responded to his enemies with compassion. It is true that he confronted them about their hypocrisy, but he did so as an expression of care and concern.

> *The natural human responses to rejection are retaliation or retreat, neither of which is a kingdom response.*

Watching Jesus live out the Beatitudes throughout the three years of his ministry must have been awe-inspiring and amazing. He never wavered because he was the "man for others." The welfare and spiritual growth of others were always more important to him than how they treated him.

By his example and teaching Jesus exalted mercy as one of the most important qualities required by God. He wanted his followers, also, to show **compassion.** Notice verse 36 and then read verse 35. Surprising, amazing, and maybe somewhat exasperating, wouldn't you say?

1. Why would Jesus assume that his followers would have enemies, haters, cursers, and abusers?

2. Is it possible for a brother or sister in Christ to be your enemy?

    What steps toward reconciliation does scripture give? See Matthew 5:21-24; 18:15-17.

3. What examples can you cite from scripture of exceptional, undeserved kindness and mercy?

4. What does each of these scriptures teach about the role of forgiveness in conflict resolution?

    Matthew 18:21-22

    Mark 11:24-26

    2 Corinthians 2:7-10

    Ephesians 4:32

5. What might be the relationship between Acts 7:55-8:1 and Acts 26:12-14?

WHAT IT MEANS

LESSON ELEVEN

The standard Jesus set for his followers in these verses is incredibly demanding, almost to the point of being unreasonable. Was he just trying to make things tough for us to weed out the weaklings? Not at all. He could set no other standard if we are to be *"sons of the Most High."* Our Father is kind to the ungrateful and wicked; he is also merciful (vv. 35-36). If God were to be kind and merciful only to those who are his equal or better in righteousness, all of us would be in deep trouble. Since he responds with **compassion** to the unrighteous, so ought we if we are to be his children.

From a strategic standpoint for the kingdom this makes a lot of sense. It is commonly accepted in the world that we have the right to defend ourselves and our property against assault and thievery. Doing so, however, tells the offender that our possessions and well-being are more important than the offender is. No kingdom of love and reconciliation can be built that way. Eye-for-an-eye ethics will only create a society of suspicious, protective, insular citizens. A paraphrase of Gandhi suggests that if everyone were to live by the eye-for-an-eye code, there would be no one to lead the rest of us about. The eye-for-an-eye prescription was not given to the Jews for personal, vengeful use. It was given to the judges as a legal guideline for regulating society. That is why Jesus reversed the injunction in Matthew 5:38-42.

> *If everyone were to live by the eye-for-an-eye code, there would be no one to lead the rest of us about.*

6. What is the underlying motive or attitude in each of these responses to rejection?

    Retreat
    Retaliation
    Restraint

7. What comes to mind when you think about the quality of **compassion**?

    Share an example or illustration of **compassion** in action.

    Why is **compassion** an important value for disciples?

8. How would you defend Christianity from the accusation of being a crutch for weak people?

    How can one be a **compassionate** Christian without appearing to be a "wimp"?

9. How does the quality of objectivity help in responding to rejection? How can one overcome anger and other negative emotion and replace it with objectivity and **compassion**?

10. What do you think about the economics of Luke 6:29-34?

Why does Jesus want us to live this way?

Share any experiences or examples of such generosity.

WHAT IT MEANS FOR ME

LESSON TWELVE

We often hear talk of the difference between objectivity and subjectivity. The latter—subjectivity—typically comes across as mostly emotional and self-focused, leaving the impression that objectivity is mostly rational. You may find it helpful to think of objectivity as seeing things as God sees them. This understanding of objectivity implies a definite sense of reality—seeing things as they really are. It also brings with it the compassion of the loving God, who created both you and your enemy or tormentor, and died to redeem both of you.

If you outline what Jesus says in this passage, the list looks ominous. He commands us to:

- love our enemies
- do good to those who hate us
- bless those who curse us
- pray for those who mistreat us
- allow someone to strike us without retaliating
- give our shirt to a thief who steals our coat
- give to those who ask, and those who take
- lend to enemies not expecting repayment
- be merciful
- not judge or condemn others
- forgive others

These are all commands, not recommendations. Jesus said in another setting, *"You are my friends if you do what I command"* (John 15:14). And, *"If you hold to my teaching, you are really my disciples"* (John 8:31). To be a friend and a disciple of Jesus we must obey him, which includes responding to rejection and abuse with **compassion** and kindness.

11. Which three of these commands above would you find it most difficult to obey?

12. Can you identify a person who because of your Christian stand (name him/her):

Is your enemy?

Hates you?

Curses you?

Mistreats you?

What has been your response to these people?

What should it be?

It may be helpful for the group members to hold each other accountable for responding biblically (Luke 6:27-28) to these people. Pray about it with each other week to week.

13. What is the role of the church in helping Christians respond to enemies, haters, cursers, and abusers?

14. How will the distinction between wants and needs affect the way we respond to those who ask or try to take from us?

15. How can we make the Golden Rule (v. 31) work for us? That is, how can it really become our first instinct in relationships?

Pray with each other to grow in the area of **compassion.**

NOW WHAT?

Kingdom Strategy # 4

In kingdom living, disciples of Jesus Christ respond to hostility and rejection by treating their enemies as well as they want to be treated themselves.

Go back to question 12 in Lesson Twelve. Review your answers. If you left these questions blank, think more deeply about it. If you still cannot identify anyone who is abusive toward you in attitude or action, is it because you have not taken a firm stand for Christ?

Assuming there is someone who despises you because of your Christian commitment, recall the last encounter you had with that person, and tell the group about it. Include an honest appraisal about how you responded to the other person's abuse or rejection of you. Ask the group if you handled it correctly.

Now the difficult part: reveal to the group how you honestly feel about that person.

> *Are you willing to become part of God's answer to your prayer?*

Now visualize or speculate what that person might be like if s/he were a disciple of Jesus Christ. What strengths and gifts would he or she bring to the work of the Lord? Can you now pray for him or her, asking God to bring into reality what you have just imagined? Are you willing to become part of God's answer to your prayer? How might the bad feelings between the two of you be used redemptively by God? Are you willing to continue to suffer this person's scorn, wrath, or abuse quietly while loving and praying him or her into the kingdom?

Discuss these questions with the people in your group, and enter your responses and interactions with this person into your journal each week. Hold each other accountable for loving your enemy.

If your enemy is a brother or sister in Christ, review the principles suggested in the scriptures listed in question twelve. What is the direction of the anger?

    a) you → him/her

    b) he/she → you

    c) you ← → him/her

If a) or c), what stops you from forgiving him or her? Must he or she be reproved according to Matthew 18:15-17? If so, ask the people in your group to help you begin this process. If not, you have no other basis for not forgiving your brother. Ask the members of your group to pray with you confessing your forgiveness, and then determine to go to your enemy-brother seeking reconciliation.

If b), do you know why the other person is angry with you? Have you tried to make things right according to Matthew 5:23-24? Would it be helpful to have someone in your group go with you to help solve the conflict?

If c), and the two of you are at an impasse, that is, you disagree on who is at fault and both expect the other one to make it right, would you submit to the collective wisdom and counsel of your group? If they agree with you that the other person must make restitution and seek reconciliation, covenant to pray for the person, and see if a third party might speak with him or her about it. If your group believes you must take action to settle the issue, submit to their counsel.

CHAPTER FIVE

EXAMINING MYSELF

Disciple Quality: **INTEGRITY**

WHAT IT SAYS

LESSON THIRTEEN
Read Luke 6:37-49

Jesus gave three distinct emphases in this sermon found in Luke 6. Verses 17-26 address the inner attitudes of the disciple, which we have summarized with the word "humility." In verses 27-36 Jesus counseled his followers about responding to enemies; we have used the quality compassion to communicate that teaching.

Another shift of emphasis begins in verse 37. A fellow-disciple, or a brother, is the focus here; the teaching is that we are to be very patient with one another. We are to be gracious, generous, and full-hearted in our acceptance of brothers and sisters in the faith. This kind of response is fitting for us because we know that we also often need to be forgiven (v.37), we also are blind (v.39), and we also have a plank in our eye (v.41).

We capture this character quality with the word **integrity** because it means being honest with yourself so that your standards for others will be no higher than for yourself. By examining ourselves first, we will not be hyper-critics (v.42).

1. How are the alternatives of judging and forgiving others illustrated in Luke 6:47-49?

2. Is eye-for-eye ethics as taught in the Old Testament consistent with Jesus' teaching about not judging others? If not, how can we explain the inconsistency?

3. If you had witnessed the events in John 8:1-11, what do you think your response might have been?

   ____ Moral outrage at the woman's sin

   ____ Zeal to obey the Law

   ____ Compassion for the woman

   ____ Anger at the Pharisees

   ____ Consciousness of your own faults

   ____ Surprise at the leniency of Jesus

   Why do you think Jesus wrote on the ground?

   What do you think Jesus wrote on the ground?

4. Paul said "No"; Barnabas said "Yes" to John Mark's desire to be reinstated for missionary service. Was Paul guilty of judging Mark? Why or why not?

   Is it possible that neither Paul nor Barnabas was wrong in their decision? Explain.

   What do you think is the key to making such a decision about someone else's qualifications?

   Do you think Paul's request years later (2 Timothy 4:11) indicates he thought he had made the wrong choice?

WHAT IT MEANS

LESSON FOURTEEN

This section contains one of the texts often used by preachers,

> *Give, and it will be given unto you. A good measure, pressed down, shaken together and running over, will be poured into your lap. (Luke 6:38)*

We naturally assume Jesus was talking about financial giving. How many stewardship sermons have you heard based on this text? Look more closely at the context. Jesus was not talking about money, but about forgiveness. Using today's terminology, what we are supposed to give is the benefit of the doubt. God has not called

> *God has not called us to be referees, running along the sideline ready to throw a penalty flag or blow the whistle on others.*

us to be referees, running along the sideline ready to throw a penalty flag or blow the whistle, calling fouls or penalties on others. Instead, we are to be aware of our own need for forgiveness and be generous in offering our forgiveness to others.

The remainder of verse 38 makes that clear, *For with the measure you use, it will be measured unto you*. The imagery is of grain being poured into one's tunic pouch, but the reference is to forgiveness. Your standard (measure) of harshness or leniency will be the standard others (or God?) will use for you.

5. How can one be realistic and honest about sin and failure without judging?

   How can we avoid judging (v.37), while at the same time being alert to *bad trees* and *bad fruit* (vv. 43-44)?

6. What does the word **integrity** suggest to you?

   How is this quality basic to all other character qualities?

7. Chapter 5 of *"Follow Me"* tells the story of a man who judged a minister who wore outlandish bracelets. Can you share an episode in your life when you misjudged someone?

8. In which kind of circumstances might it be right to reveal to another person his faults?

WHAT IT MEANS FOR ME

LESSON FIFTEEN

This passage also contains one of the most important verses undergirding the MasterWorks philosophy of discipleship:

> *A student (disciple, <u>mathetes</u> in Greek) is not above his teacher, but everyone who is fully trained will be like his teacher. (Luke 6:40)*

> *The most important aspect about being a disciple is whose disciple we are.*

You may recall that in the Introduction to *"Follow Me"* we emphasized that the essence of being a disciple of Jesus Christ is becoming like him in character. That is why Jesus focused almost all his efforts with his followers on teaching them about character qualities. And that is why the fifteen chapters of *"Follow Me"* and the chapters of this Group Guide emphasize character qualities, not abilities, personality, training, activity, or behavior.

Becoming like the teacher in character is the essence of discipleship. If we become disciples of a blind guide, he will lead us into a pit with himself. Many today are following personalities and philosophies of life that will surely lead into the pit. The most important aspect about being a disciple is whose disciple we are. As we sit under the tutelage of Jesus, we will be gaining his perspective on life, and our responses to problems, opportunities, relationships, and circumstances will be like his. When we are fully trained, we will be like him. We will embody all the character qualities we are studying, and that includes the one in this chapter: **integrity**.

9. As you observe other people, about which kinds of failures or inadequacies are you most prone to be critical or judgmental?

10. In judging ourselves, the extremes of introspection are self-blindness (indulgence) on the one side, and spiritual paranoia (legalism) on the other side. Toward which are you more prone? (Circle an arrow to indicate.)

    <— — —   — — —>
    self-blindness   proper introspection   spiritual paranoia

    What steps can you take to achieve perfect balance?

11. If you have read Chapter 5 of "*Follow Me*", you may recall the Pygmalion Principle. The idea is that one person who really believes in another can have tremendous impact in building strength, confidence and ability in another person far more than the other person would have believed. Has there been someone in your life who has exemplified this principle? How did it affect you?

    How is the Pygmalion concept emphasized in Ephesians 6:4 and Colossians 3:21, especially for family men?

12. Do you know someone who is a "diamond in the rough," a person with great potential who needs to be encouraged rather than be judged?

    Are you in a position to help that person?

13. Discuss the possibility and challenge of being accountable to one another as disciples without being judgmental. How is integrity key to this dynamic?

NOW WHAT?

Kingdom Strategy #5

Rather than focusing on the failures and inadequacies of others, disciples of Christ periodically engage in healthy self-evaluation to assess their own spiritual status.

Too often, unchurched people label churchgoers as hypocrites, and they are right. The world has only two kinds of people: hypocrites and forgiven hypocrites. The teaching of Jesus about judging should not discourage us from having high standards; rather, it should prompt us to see the failures of others as reminders to examine ourselves.

Having a plank in my eye obviously disqualifies me from extracting a speck from another person's eye. The ultimate irony is that after I have extracted my own plank, it is likely that the speck in the other's eye will no longer be visible to me. What I thought was his speck may have been my plank all along.

A teacher who was tired of using chalkboard and eraser in the classroom decided to go high tech one day and use a power point. Captivated by his own lesson and wanting to change a word, he picked up the eraser and began wiping the wall. When the students laughed, he sensed his foolish act, went to the projector, and made the erasure on the data slide. The word was no longer on the wall! How often are we critical of the wall when in reality we are projecting the very thing that needs to be changed!

> *Do we not often view others as competitors to whom we must show ourselves to be superior?*

To nail down the teaching on integrity, let's take a look deep inside, right to the core of our souls. Why do we judge others? Is it not because in our fallen nature we are insecure about our own **integrity**? Do we not often view others as competitors to whom we must show ourselves to be superior? Young children, still insecure about their parents' love for them, compete with their siblings by constant insults and put-downs. We are not much different. You may want to discuss these issues with your group.

a. If you are keeping a spiritual journal, focus for one week, or one day, on the occasions and people where you have been critical or judgmental. Note if or why you felt justified in your criticism. Then try to determine what insecurity of yours might have motivated your response.

b. Who are your competitors? Name them. How are you threatened by them? Is there a useful role that competitors can play in your life? How might you turn a competitor into a colleague?

c. By now, perhaps you are planning to become a disciple-maker by starting another group. This may be a good time to take a break, having completed the first unit. During the break, perhaps one or more of your group will want to start another group, and then continue also in this group when it starts again. This is the best way to multiply disciples.

Here is an **integrity** check before you proceed. How would you anticipate your ability to build up other people using the eight applications of the Pygmalion Principle found in Chapter 5 of *"Follow Me"*? Rate yourself on each one. Do not expect perfection before you are ready to disciple others, but look for growth and the intention to be a people builder.

REVIEW

With this study of integrity, we've reached the end of the first section of the *"Follow Me"* Materials, having studied the first five character qualities Jesus sought to instill in his disciples. In the *"Follow Me"* text we have grouped these five qualities together under the title *Learning Kingdom Values*. These five qualities are foundational to the teachings that follow.

Notice the characteristics of qualities like teachability, flexibility and humility, right at the beginning of Jesus' teaching ministry. These qualities are tied directly to a willingness to listen, heed, and obey. Willingness to obey is foundational; according to John 8:31-32 it is the basis for knowing the truth. It is also key to abiding in God's love, and having unity with God's people.

It is essential to know, however, that Christian disciples are not called upon to obey a set of rules and regulations. We are called to obey Jesus. And to do that, we must remain (or abide) in him. See John 15 to see how important this idea is for Jesus.

One of the dangers of focusing on character qualities is that, unless we seek to deepen our walk with Jesus, we may find ourselves on a self-improvement track. The goal of discipleship is not self-improvement, but Christ-likeness.

- Try to identify an episode from the life of Jesus where he modeled each of the five qualities we have studied thus far, and as objectively as possible, assess your development or progress in this area (using 1-5, with 5 being the best).

Discipleship Quality	Example from Jesus	My Progress
Teachability		
Flexibility		
Humility		
Compassion		
Integrity		

- When you are finished with your individual self-assessments, take turns in your group sharing your personal perspectives on yourselves. Then, carefully and thoughtfully, give one another feedback.

When you are giving feedback, make every effort to be specific, to describe actual behaviors you have observed and statements you've heard. Avoid imputing a motive, assuming that you know what the other person was thinking or feeling at the time. Let the other person talk about his or her motives, if appropriate.

When it is your turn to receive feedback, make every effort to listen to the specific observations. Ask questions for clarification, but resist the temptation to defend, explain or justify.

Where appropriate, work together to identify specific steps a person may need to consider taking to solve a dilemma, improve a relationship, or build a new approach to difficult situations.

- Based on that activity, what have you learned about giving feedback with integrity?
- What have you learned about your own receptivity (teachability) to having your own behavior "judged" or assessed by a friend?
- By now you have realized that the *"Follow Me"* strategy for making disciples is peer-oriented. That is, the members of your group are discipling one another under the authority of Jesus and his Word. Discuss the possibility and challenge of being accountable to one another as disciples without being judgmental. How are teachability, flexibility, humility, compassion and integrity strategic to this dynamic?
- Pray together about your continuing growth as disciples of Jesus Christ. Where needed, make individual commitments to be accountable and to check with one another.

UNIT TWO

LEARNING KINGDOM MINISTRY
Being a Disciple in the World

Selflessness	Intensity
Courage	Dependency
Transparency	Contentment

CHAPTER SIX

KNOWING HIS LORDSHIP

Disciple Quality: **SELFLESSNESS**

WHAT IT SAYS

LESSON SIXTEEN
Read Luke 9:18-27

This event at Caesarea Philippi is considered by many New Testament scholars to be a pivotal point in the ministry of Jesus. The bold, straightforward declaration made by Peter, testifying to his belief in Jesus as Messiah, changed the focus of the ministry of Jesus. Up to this point he was exercising spiritual power in support of his teaching about the kingdom of God. He was viewed as perhaps a bit eccentric, but a fairly harmless fellow.

Once Jesus knew his chosen Twelve believed in his messiahship, he began a more vigorous campaign of denouncing the spiritual corruption of Judaism. He also spent more time teaching the Twelve the more demanding implications of being a disciple of the kingdom of God. Matthew's account (Matthew 16:21) makes this change of tactics even more clear,

> *<u>From that time on</u> Jesus began to explain to his disciples that he must go to Jerusalem and suffer many things at the hands of the elders, chief priests and teachers of the law. . . (emphasis added).*

All of this suggests that the strategy of Jesus from the very beginning was to train and motivate a small group of men to whom he could entrust the future of his church. So Peter's declaration was a strategic moment in the life of the church.

The truth of the identity of Jesus is one of the absolutes of the Christian faith. Any view of him short of full belief in him as Messiah and Son of the Living God (Matthew 16:16) is not Christian. Millions of people and thousands of groups are ready to pay respect and honor to Jesus, much like the crowds who considered him to be a prophet. But confront these people with the unique messianic deity of Jesus and they will want no part of it. For the disciple of Jesus there can be no hesitation, no wavering, no compromise, no doubt about the unique status of Jesus as God's one and only Son sent to the world as the

> *For the disciple of Jesus there can be no hesitation, no wavering, no compromise, no doubt about the unique status of Jesus as God's one and only Son sent to the world.*

anointed Messiah of Israel and Savior of all those who put their trust in him. Short of this, one cannot be a disciple; neither can one be a Christian.

The call to discipleship may indeed come before one's confession of faith, but the implications of it will not be welcomed or even tolerated without this belief. John 6:60-69 shows this clearly. Many so-called disciples abandoned Jesus when he began to give *"a hard teaching."* Peter responded for the Twelve when Jesus asked if they also wanted to leave,

Lord, to whom shall we go? You have the words of eternal life. We believe and know that you are the Holy One of God. (John 6:68-69)

1. What did the opinions of the crowd reveal about their understanding of Jesus?

   What are some of the more commonly held ideas about Jesus among the non-Christians you know?

2. What truths are implied in our text about the identity of Jesus, who he is and who or what he is not?

   What truths about our identity are in the passage?

3. Which phrase best describes how Peter perceived Jesus?

   a. A national savior and hero

   b. The long-awaited anointed one

   c. The leader of spiritual renewal

   d. An exciting, insightful new rabbi

4. Why do you think Jesus used the terms *"lose"* and *"forfeit"*? What is the difference?

   Does this passage and do these two words suggest anything about eternal security?

5. What is your understanding of Paul's simple, but often used phrase *"in Christ?"* How does this concept give extra meaning to Luke 9:23-24?

WHAT IT MEANS

LESSON SEVENTEEN

In the text for this lesson, Jesus warns about the prospect of gaining the whole world, but losing one's soul. People planning the "hostile takeover" of a business venture start out by buying small amounts of the stock of the company they intend to acquire. That way they don't tip their hand too early. In much the same way, we are tempted to sell off our soul piece by piece, one small incident, one convenient rationalization after another.

A little bit at a time, we can give up our integrity in exchange for temporary gains. Once started, the practice can become habitual until one day you wake up and realize that you have sacrificed your very self, and in return have received ashes.

The paradox of losing your life (or soul; the Greek word is *psyche*) if you try to keep it, and saving it if you lose it for Jesus shows that it is not just Jesus' identity that is in question. The point of the paradox is that apart from Jesus we have no lasting identity. By investing our passion, energy, and resources in struggling to be someone and insure our own immortality, we in fact achieve the opposite. This struggle of the soul is the most elemental expression of sin. It is the human competing with God rather than cooperating with him. Acknowledging God's right to own and control my life is best described as **selflessness.**

6. Why is the identity of Jesus the most basic and important issue for a disciple?

    Why did Jesus wait before he began to reveal his identity?

7. Share an example of the person you know who best exemplifies verse 23.

8. What might Henri Nouwen, in *Reaching Out*[iv], mean by going beyond:

    Loneliness to solitude

    Hostility to hospitality

    Illusion to prayer

9. What does it mean to lose your life, verse 24? Does it have to do with personal worth? self esteem? all your rights? the "good life"? the lower nature? self image? your identity?

    Why is **selflessness** fundamental to effective Kingdom ministry?

10. How might non-Christians attack the logic of verse 25?

    How would you respond?

WHAT IT MEANS FOR ME

LESSON EIGHTEEN

The importance of the saying in verse 24 is clear from the frequent use Jesus made of it in one form or another. He used it in the charge to the Twelve (Matthew 10:39), the first prediction of his death and resurrection (Matthew 16:25; Mark 8:35; Luke 9:24), the teaching on the coming of the kingdom (Luke 17:33), and the response to the inquiring Greeks (John 12:25). The logic of the saying is expressed in verse 25 by noting the extreme consequences of the two choices. The maximum prize of the one seeking to live without regard to Christ is gaining the whole world, an offer Jesus turned down during the temptation (see Luke 4:5-8), but the price is one's very soul, i.e. the eternal part of his being. By inference, one who gives his life to the cause of Christ may not gain much of this world, but he will not lose his soul.

It might be thought that Jesus was here giving a lesson in shrewd investment, short-term loss for long-term gain. Such is not the case because that would be simply a more intense type of selfish ambition. The previous verse shows that Jesus was not talking about investment and not even sacrifice, but liquidation—a complete sell out. The word "deny" is a strong term that means "forget that (you) exist," or "cease to consider (your) own interests in the slightest degree." And the meaning of the word "cross" is painfully clear. A cross is not a burden; it is a death machine. One carries a cross only to be executed on it. The punishment is not the carrying but the crucifixion.

> *Jesus was not talking about investment and not even sacrifice, but liquidation—a complete sell out.*

The demand of Jesus is daily crucifixion of selfish interest. Although gaining one's soul eternally is the result of following Christ this way, it is not to be the motive. The motive is not gain, but godliness. We obey not because of the personal profit, but because he is God and we are his creatures. Our submission is totally appropriate; rebellion is totally worthy of condemnation.

11. If Jesus asked you, *"Who do you say that I am?,"* in all honesty, what would your answer be?

12. What are some practical ways that we can take up our cross daily and follow Jesus?

13. As you ponder the idea of denying yourself, which of these concerns will die the hardest?

____ Your reputation   ____ Your sharp tongue

____ Your use of leisure   ____ Your financial status

____ Your hopes and dreams   ____ Your family's future

____ Your wounds   ____ Other

14. How do we sometimes show we are "ashamed" of Jesus and his words?

    Probably all of us have denied Jesus at one time or another. In what kind of situation is it most difficult for you not to be ashamed of Jesus?

15. By the standards Jesus set forth in verses 23-26, which best describes you? Ready to follow Jesus:

    a. all the way   b. most of the way

    c. some of the way   d. none of the way

Pray for each other to grow in the area of **selflessness.**

NOW WHAT?

Kingdom Strategy #6

Disciples must put the cause of the kingdom in priority over their own happiness, convenience, comfort, and even their own existence.

Way back in the Garden of Eden the first question God asked Adam was, *"Where are you?"* Adam's response was, *"I heard you in the garden, and I was afraid because I was naked; so I hid."* (Genesis 3:9-10) He was not just physically naked; he was suddenly transparent, totally exposed as a sinner. Adam and Eve hid so well that they could not even find themselves. And that has been our problem all these years. We have hidden ourselves from the Source of life. And without him we cannot find ourselves.

Jesus gives us a clue to this whole problem. It is also part of the answer to another question: "What is a disciple?" The answer is found in Luke 9: We will only find ourselves when we lose ourselves in Christ. Jesus was not talking here about losing our identity, our personality, our individuality, or our personhood. Underline the syllable *self* in verse 23, and you will understand what he meant. It is the self-centeredness, self-absorption, and the selfish interests that need to be denied. If not, you will lose your life; that is, your future is dead-ended. Why? Because apart from Christ, you have no future beyond your death. And apart from Christ, life does not make sense. As one dropout said, "Life is a joke and I'm the punch line."

Perhaps most difficult to accept is the death of our reputation, our respectability. Thus Jesus warned his followers about being ashamed of him, his way, and his words. In a naturalistic, rationalistic world, people who live for and die for a king who cannot be seen—a king who was crucified on a cross and whose power is seen in denial and death of self—will be held up for ridicule, persecution, and ostracism. It will be no different for the student than for the Master. As Bonhoeffer said, "When Christ calls a man, he bids him come and die."

In Chapter Eight you will be focusing on courage as the kingdom quality for disciples. The gist of the lesson is that the gospel must be demonstrated as well as proclaimed. The emphasis will be on demonstrating the gospel in practical action, especially as group activity. We will be suggesting a way your group can become a mission group. In preparation for that, it may be helpful

> *Your goal is to get people to declare themselves on the issue of the identity of Jesus Christ.*

now for your group to devise a questionnaire which will take you into conversations with non-Christians about the identity of Jesus.

Remember the questions Jesus asked his disciples to elicit their beliefs regarding his identity?

- *Who do men say that I am?*
- *Who do you say that I am?*

Using that model, work out a prototype of a dialogue you will be able to use with others. Begin with questions and plan responses to the various possible answers you might get. Work key scripture verses into your presentation. Your goal is to get people to declare themselves on the issue of the identity of Jesus, and then to help them come to the truth about who he is and make an appropriate response. For those who have the right answer, try to determine whether they are living obediently as his disciples. You may want to try out your script on each other in the group before using it in public.

A good bridge between **selflessness** and **courage** is the story of Queen Esther. She was truly one of the heroines of biblical days. Chosen from among hundreds to be queen of the Persian king in place of the petulant Queen Vashti. In the midst of a most stressful situation, Esther declared the famous words, *"If I perish, I perish"* (Esther 4:16). To this day, many Jews celebrate the Feast of Purim in recognition of Esther's **selflessness** and **courage**.

If all in your group are not familiar with this wonderful story, an edifying exercise would be to have someone tell the story after reviewing the ten chapters of the book of Esther.

Could modern-day Persia (Iran) be building its own "gallows" these days?

CHAPTER SEVEN

FOCUSING ON PRIORITIES

Disciple Quality: **INTENSITY**

WHAT IT SAYS

LESSON NINETEEN
Read Luke 9:57-62

Jesus and his disciples were walking along the road. Where were they going? What was their destination? Was there any particular direction to this walk? Luke tells us (vs. 51) they were heading for Jerusalem. His **intensity** is evident: *Jesus resolutely set out for Jerusalem* (or *Jesus set his face like a flint toward Jerusalem*). But there would be many stops along the way.

For Jesus, the question of where was always less important than the question of why. Why was Jesus going? The next chapter indicates he was going to recruit more disciples whom he could send to prepare the way for him to minister in the trans-Jordan area. In one sense, which road he was on was irrelevant; more important for him was finding qualified disciples. You see, Jesus lived with intentionality (purpose, direction). And intentionality is the parent of **intensity. Intensity** without intentionality is mere busyness.

Jesus never hid from a disciple the opportunity to count the cost. Only those who entered his service with eyes wide open would be useful disciples. Is it not the same today? As a youth pastor during the latter years (1972-74) of the Jesus People days, I was often encouraged to see promising young people respond to the challenge of becoming a One Way, counter culture Jesus Freak. Some of them stuck it out. Many of them did not. As long as the movement was popular, they were glad to be hiking with Jesus, even though they had no clue where or why he was headed. When the thrill of the fad faded, so did their dedication.

As we enter this chapter of lessons on **intensity**, we must seek to know where and why Jesus is going in our lives. The first of the three would-be disciples said he would follow Jesus *"wherever you go."* Wherever, but maybe not whyever. Perhaps he thought it was neat to be hiking with Jesus—wherever. Little did he know that the hike would soon take the disciples across the Jordan to proclaim the kingdom in enemy territory—whyever.

1. How did the events in Luke 9:48-50 and 51-55 help train the disciples for their upcoming mission (Luke 10)?

2. Does verse 50 seem to contradict the way Jesus responded to the three men in verses 57-62? Explain.

3. Where do you think the three men thought Jesus was going (cf. vv. 51-52), and what might they have been expecting?

4. Was Jesus' response to the first man (v.57) motivated by special insight into the man's potential weakness, or by Jesus' desire to give full disclosure about the rigors of following?

    If the former, should we be somewhat fussy about whom we recruit for discipleship or service?

5. Where in these verses and the surrounding verses do you see the **intensity** of Jesus?

    Why does it seem that **intensity** was the character quality Jesus was teaching his disciples through these encounters?

WHAT IT MEANS

LESSON TWENTY

What is the direction of your life? Are you just aimlessly rambling around, filling the time? For the disciple of Jesus, purposeful, directed living is possible and expected. The clue to such a fulfilling life is understanding the goals and purposes of the Master. But as you learn more about his agenda, don't be shocked. Life with Jesus is not a Sunday stroll. His goal takes us to, onto, and beyond the cross.

> *Christian disciples are, by definition, counter-cultural...our first allegiance is not to any human culture in this world.*

Christian disciples are, by definition, counter-cultural. That is, our first allegiance is not to any human culture in this world. In so-called "free" societies it may be easy, even "cool," to appear to be counter-cultural, but in many parts of the world disciples of Jesus pay a huge price for putting their faith ahead of their patriotism.

Jesus, of course, was the most counter-cultural person to walk this earth. In fact, so committed was he to the kingdom of God that he paid for it with his life. He calls all who would follow him to be counter-cultural also, to *seek first the kingdom of heaven* (Matthew 6:33). It is also his will that we all learn to minister counter-culturally. The Great Commission (see Matthew 28:19-20 and Acts 1: 8) tells us to take the gospel to all cultures. Followers who are willing to obey that command are the kind of disciples Jesus still seeks. They embrace the **intensity** needed to get the job done.

Risk taking, acting on faith, is the **intensity** part of discipleship. Clearly, the three men in our text were not risk takers; apparently, comfort, propriety, and approval meant too much to them. As you ponder their stories in the next three lessons, you may become uncomfortable. Your own **intensity** level will be challenged, but keep your hand to the plow. There's no harvest without plowing.

6. How would going through Samaria prepare the disciples for cross-cultural ministry?

    Why does cross cultural ministry demand greater **intensity** than other ministry?

    Tell about the ministry occasion when you have had to reach the farthest from your comfort zone.

7. What are some biblical words or phrases that support **intensity** as a spiritual quality?

    Who are some biblical models of **intensity**?

    Why is kingdom **intensity** key to effective ministry?

8. Based on their conversations with Jesus, which of the three men was the best candidate for discipleship?

9. What seemed to be lacking in these three men?

    Why did Jesus not just accept them as they were and plan to change them?

10. Do you think the three men in our text could have chosen not to follow Jesus and yet have been (or become) Christians?

    If so, is there a double standard in Christianity?

    If not, is it really all or nothing for Jesus? What about justification by faith, not works?

WHAT IT MEANS FOR ME

LESSON TWENTY-ONE

Intensity with intentionality (would you prefer "passion with purpose"?) may not seem to be a spiritual quality. Isn't the same characteristic essential for success in business or any profession? Of course it is. Should that disqualify it for being essential for kingdom work? Some think that spiritual work is just praying and waiting on God.

A seminary professor, speaking to a board of trustees, shared the following idea. He said as a young man he yearned to experience the power of God in his life and ministry. In church he had been taught that the power of God comes through much prayer and waiting on God. So he prayed. And he prayed, and he waited. No power of God. Eventually he decided to see for himself what scripture says about the power of God. As he analyzed the stories of God's mighty acts, he was shocked to find that God unleashes his power as people take risks, not while they are still safely on their knees. On our knees we find out what to do, but the power does not come until we start doing. The old hymn title has it right: "Trust and Obey." Trusting without obeying is like inhaling without exhaling. It doesn't get the job done.

> *God unleashes his power as people take risks.*

11. Who is the most intense person you know?

    What are the good and bad features about this quality?

    How can **intensity** be channeled in positive directions?

12. Before you became a disciple, how informed were you about where Jesus is going and what it would mean to follow him?

    Did you count the cost?

    What surprise turns in the road have you experienced?

13. What might Jesus have said to you if you had volunteered in the same way as the first man?

    Would this really be an objection by Jesus or an excuse you might use?

14. Which of the three statements Jesus used is the greatest challenge to your discipleship?

    ____ *Foxes have holes. . .* (comfort)

    ____ *Let the dead bury their own dead. . .* (social propriety)

    ____ *No one who puts his hand to the plow. . .* (approval)

    Why?

    What is the real issue in each case?

15. What would your friends say about your **intensity** level?

    What would you say about your **intensity** as a disciple?

16. How can we grow in our **intensity**?

    If **intensity** in following Jesus is an area of needed growth in your life, who might be able to help you?

    Will you ask that person to help you design an approach for growing in intensity?

    Pray for each other to grow in the area of **intensity.**

NOW WHAT?

Kingdom Strategy # 7

Discipleship demands singleness of purpose, which will be demonstrated by a sense of extreme urgency for advancing God's kingdom.

Our Lord's earthly life was a study in righteous **intensity**. At age twelve, when his earthly parents left him behind in Jerusalem, Jesus was already ordering his priorities toward the work of God. When confronted by Mary and Joseph, who had anxiously looked for him for three days, he responded, *"Did you not know that I must be about my Father's business?"* (Luke 2:49, NKJB). This mission was later succinctly defined with these words: *"The Son of Man came to seek and to save what was lost"* (Luke 19:10). Luke also tells us *"As the time approached for him to be taken up to heaven, Jesus resolutely set out for Jerusalem"* (Luke 9:51). In Isaiah's prophecy, this fierce determination is expressed picturesquely in our Redeemer's own words: *"Because the Sovereign Lord helps me, I will not be disgraced. Therefore I have set my face like a flint. . ."* (Isaiah 50:7).

The most triumphant words uttered by our Savior were also the last before he died: *"It is finished"* (John 19:30). The **intensity** of Jesus in pursuing his God-given purpose on earth is evident throughout the Gospels, but it accurately reflects the **intensity** of God the Father, whose plan of redemption was set in motion immediately after the fall and will continue through history until its consummation with the return of Christ to set up his kingdom in full.

The unswerving clarity of focus that is part of his own character is a kingdom quality Jesus looks for in his disciples. The top priority for a disciple should be the advancement of God's kingdom.

One of the goals of discipleship is to learn our place in kingdom service. Why has Jesus called me? How has he gifted me? What motivations has he given me, i.e., what is my life's message? For a full treatment of *charismata* see *Walking in Your Anointing* by David E. Schroeder.

It may come as no great surprise to you that people are most intense about what they believe in most and what they do best. This is true in all areas of life, including our discipleship. Therefore, knowing our spiritual gift and life's message is vitally important. As we understand how God has motivated us and what message or method he has given us, we will be far more intense about our service for him.

Now this could get complicated and move well outside the scope of this lesson. Spiritual gifts is a controversial topic in the body of Christ. For our purposes we will consider only the most basic list of spiritual gifts, which is found in Romans 12:6-8. Seven gifts are found there, and by studying the words and noting how they are used in other passages, we can get a fairly full understanding of them. While other ministries and manifestations of the Holy Spirit are available to believers, each Christian has (at least) one of these gifts. A much more thorough presentation of spiritual gifts and manifestations of the Spirit is given in David Schroeder's book *Walking in Your Anointing*, available through MasterWorks (email to: info@masterworksinc.org).

If you do not already know your spiritual gift, perhaps this exercise will help you. One of the benefits of being in a small group of people who know you well is their ministry in confirming what your gift is. Peter (1 Peter 4:10-11) reduces all the spiritual gifts to speaking and serving gifts, and those found in Romans 12 fit this pattern. (Empathizing may be either a speaking or a serving gift.) Below is a listing of the gifts with phrases indicating the motivation and message (speaking gifts) or method (serving gifts) of each.

SPIRITUAL GIFT	MOTIVATION	MESSAGE / METHOD
Prophecy	Proclaim truth	"Be righteous"
Serving	Meet needs	Sacrificing
Teaching	Clarify truth	"Be truthful"
Exhorting	Stimulate growth	"Be mature"
Giving	Entrust assets	Investing
Organizing	Coordinate efforts	Delegating
Empathizing	Give comfort	"Be well"

Here are some questions that will help you determine your gift and be able to serve Christ more intensely in that gift.

1. In ministering for Christ, which gives you greater fulfillment: speaking or serving? If speaking, look for your gift to be prophecy, teaching, exhorting, or empathizing. If serving, look for your gift to be serving, giving, organizing, or empathizing.

2. If you believe you have a speaking gift,

   a. which of these motivations seems closest to your core concern?
      * Proclaim truth (prophecy)
      * Clarify truth (teaching)
      * Stimulate growth (exhorting)
      * Give comfort (empathizing)

b. Which of these messages do you hear loudest in your soul?
   * "Be righteous" (prophecy)
   * "Be accurate" (teaching)
   * "Be mature" (exhorting)
   * "Be well" (empathizing)

3. If you believe you have a serving gift,

   a. Which of these motivations seems closest to your core concern?
      * Meet needs (serving)
      * Entrust assets (giving)
      * Coordinate efforts (organizing)
      * Give comfort (empathizing)

   b. Which of these methods do you see yourself using?
      * Sacrificing (serving)
      * Investing (giving)
      * Delegating (organizing)
      * Identifying (empathizing)

4. After narrowing down to one or two possible gifts, all members in your group should share their findings and seek to confirm or challenge those ideas.

5. If you now know your gift, you will be better able to select ministries closer to your motivation, and thereby be more intense in your service for Christ. As a group, discuss the current ministries each of you has, and analyze whether those ministries are the best employment of your gift.

CHAPTER EIGHT

DEMONSTRATING THE GOSPEL

Disciple Quality: **COURAGE**

WHAT IT SAYS

LESSON TWENTY-TWO
Read Luke 10:1-24

We've introduced in recent weeks two qualities of discipleship that are closely linked with this one. *Selflessness* is the quality that applies to choosing values and priorities that honor the Lord. *Intensity* is the logical working-out of selflessness in a single-minded devotion to activities that serve the purposes of the kingdom of God.

The world is often at odds with God's purposes and the values of his kingdom. It stands to reason, then, that a person of selfless intensity will sometimes be found in opposition to the crowd. **Courage** will be needed for those times.

The ministry of the seventy-two (or seventy, as in some translations) shows how determined Jesus was to proclaim the gospel of the kingdom throughout Palestine. The earlier mission of the Twelve (Luke 9:1-6) was conducted in Galilee. The instructions there were similar, but the results are not reported. This was a campaign to the Trans-Jordan area (east of the Jordan) in a mixed cultural environment; hence, the injunction about eating and drinking whatever was provided. For many Americans on mission trips, for example, eating foreign foods may be a good test of **courage**!

> *Here are 35 or 36 towns in which Jesus ministered on his way to Jerusalem, and we know nothing about it.*

Notice that Jesus sent them to *"every town and place where he was about to go."* They were like "advance men," preparing the people for the coming of Jesus. Several references in this passage indicate how little we really know about the ministry of Jesus. Here are 35 or 36 towns in Trans-Jordan, which Jesus ministered to on his way to Jerusalem, and we know nothing about it.

Who were these Trans-Jordan people for whom Jesus so purposefully and methodically planned this special campaign? Many in that area were Gentiles, but whether the disciples went to them we do not know. Even the Jews who lived in that region were not really part of establishment Judaism. This goes back to the tribal division of Canaan recorded in Numbers 32 when Reuben, Gad, and half of the tribe of Manasseh opted to remain east of the Jordan. From that time on, the Trans-Jordan Jews were never perceived as being in the mainstream. Nonetheless, they were still candidates for the kingdom of God.

1. What do you think was the primary purpose for the mission in our text? Consider how verses 9, 21 and 22 may relate to each other.

    How do contemporary evangelistic efforts conform to or differ from this purpose?

2. Although the instructions in Luke 10:4-11 may have been given specifically for the mission of the seventy-two, which commands or principles are important for contemporary Christian workers?

3. Jesus gave his disciples authority to do miracles. How essential are miracles to effective evangelism?

4. Discuss your views on the section "Miracles Today" in chapter eight of *"Follow Me"*. Is there consensus in your group?

    If you do not have consensus, are you able to disagree agreeably? Will disagreement paralyze you from ministering together?

WHAT IT MEANS

LESSON TWENTY-THREE

Often, the result of accomplishing a difficult mission that calls for great **courage** is overflowing joy. That is why some extreme sports addicts take such amazing risks. As athletes they do it for *perishable rewards* (1 Corinthians 9:25), but also for "the thrill of victory." Joy is the dominant emotional effect from the mission that was accomplished in the Trans-Jordan. The success of the mission of the seventy-two is evidenced by their joy as they returned with reports that *"even the demons submit to us in your name."* Perhaps the extent of their authority was a surprise to them; expelling demons was not part of their commission, as it had been for the twelve (see 9:1).

The rejoicing of Jesus (v. 21) was not focused on the successful use of spiritual power by his disciples but, as Geldenhuys[v] says, on

> ...the fact that God in His wisdom, omnipotence and love has so arranged matters that insight is given...not to those who are self-exalted and wise in their own esteem...but to those who in childlike simplicity and humility...feel their utter dependence on the Lord and accept without intellectual arrogance the truths revealed by God through Him.

The response of Jesus about seeing Satan falling like lightning from heaven is usually taken to be a metaphorical way of saying that as the demons were being cast out, Jesus was aware of the erosion of Satan's kingdom. Verse 20 fits more neatly into the context if the statement about seeing Satan fall is taken to be a warning to the seventy-two against pride. As part of the Godhead, Jesus did, in fact, see Satan fall from favor with God, which was due to pride. The joy of the disciples was not to be based on their success, but in their position with their names recorded in heaven.

Verse 22 is a great embarrassment to liberal scholars who insist that Jesus never proclaimed his own deity. Many have claimed that this verse must have been added later by the church. There is not a shred of manuscript evidence to support such a claim. Jesus was conscious of his special, unique identity as *"the Son."* And those to whom he has revealed his Sonship and who have seen the power of his kingdom at work, indeed, have *"blessed... eyes"* (v. 23).

This successful short-term missions trip surely was a precursor to how the early church would venture out into unknown, scary gentile communities, having only the power of the gospel to demonstrate the kingdom of God. As years went by, eventually the work of missions was entrusted to the Church, as we see in Acts 13, when the church at Antioch sent out Paul and Barnabas. It is enlightening and encouraging to see how the early apostles remained committed to local churches as they went about their missionary work. And eventually, local churches began to see that the very purpose of their existence was to be the missionary arm of God.

5. Who are the "Trans-Jordan" people in your community or circle of acquaintances?

   What efforts have been made to reach these people with the gospel of the kingdom?

   What difficulties or obstacles might hinder you from reaching out to them?

   Why might it take **courage** to bring the kingdom to them?

   Perhaps as a group you should decide if and how the Lord might want to send you into mission to demonstrate and proclaim his kingdom.

6. On the line below, indicate in one of the spaces with a + where you believe the church should focus its efforts and resources in promoting the kingdom of God.

   ____\\

Social action	Evangelize
Do	Talk
Demonstrate	Proclaim
Reform	Regenerate

   Now use an X to indicate where you believe the individual Christian should focus his or her efforts.

   Turning to reality, put an O where you believe your church invests its efforts and resources.

   And finally, put a * where in reality you represent the kingdom of God.

7. If the best evangelistic strategy for a local church in its own community is its corporate testimony, how do you assess your church's reputation in these four areas of ministry (Acts 2:42)?

   Grade A, B, C, D or F

   _____ The Apostles' teaching (and preaching)

   _____ Fellowship (caring and sharing)

   _____ Breaking of bread (worship and communion)

   _____ Prayer

   How does this performance impact evangelism in your area?

8. If your church receives good grades above, what efforts are being made to make this visible to the community?

   If your church receives average or poor grades above, what can your group do to help the situation?

9. Based on the above conclusions, how might the kingdom of God be better advanced in your community?

10. Share experiences you have had or heard about regarding pro-active, overt efforts made to impact a community for Christ.

WHAT IT MEANS FOR ME

LESSON TWENTY-FOUR

The seriousness of the task given to the disciples and the threat it posed are expressed in the two metaphors—they will be harvesters, far too few for the fields, and they will be as lambs among wolves. The instructions Jesus gave the seventy-two were summarized in three statements by William Barclay[vi]. They were: 1) "not to be cluttered up with material things. . ." but to "travel light;" 2) "to concentrate on (their) task;" and 3) "not be in the work for what (they could) get out of it." Their authority was directly related to Jesus. Those who received their ministry received him; those who rejected their ministry rejected him.

The mission itself was not complicated: demonstrate and announce the kingdom of God. But it was a message that required **courage** and the overcoming of natural fears.

Fear of the unknown holds many of us back from ministries to people of other cultures or strata of society. Fear of the unknown holds many of us back from a full life. As you read the Gospels, you hear Jesus repeatedly admonishing his disciples with the words, *"Don't be afraid."* Here he addresses them more bluntly with a command: *"Go, I am sending you out like lambs among wolves."* They were made of the same flesh as we are, so no doubt they too were preoccupied with safety and security. **Courage** makes for good drama in the movies, but does Jesus really intend to put disciples in danger's way? In a word, Yes. Jesus seems to be saying, "Don't worry; the worst that could happen is they'll kill you," which is, after all, what wolves do to lambs. "So, don't be afraid. Go! Go and proclaim the good news, by deeds and words."

11. Recognizing that we all will be held accountable one day for the responsible use of our gifts—the stewardship of our talents—what opportunities for demonstrating the gospel or announcing the kingdom have you shied away from out of fear?

12. How can you support and encourage one another to step out courageously, demonstrating and announcing the gospel?

    What are some of your worst fears about stepping out into the world? How does Jesus' command —*Go! I am sending you out*—come to you now?

    How might small groups be useful in undertaking special missions to demonstrate and proclaim the gospel?

13. Which other cultural identity would be most difficult for you to cross to share the gospel?

    ____ age   ____ race   ____ education

    ____ culture   ____ gender   ____ social status

14. Share with each other the most scary witnessing situation you've experienced, what you learned, and the outcome.

15. If your group wants to become a mission group, make that mission the focus of your prayer and plan each week as you continue in this MasterWorks material.

    Pray for each other to grow in the area of **courage.**

NOW WHAT?

Kingdom Strategy #8

Because the mission of the kingdom of God is accomplished by demonstration and proclamation of the gospel, when courageous disciples further that mission, they are the kingdom.

What is the mandate of modern disciples? Assuming that both demonstration and proclamation are needed to communicate the gospel effectively, how are we to proceed? Because for hundreds of years

Christians have not been able to command miracles like the seventy-two did, we have tended to have only a tell-it gospel with little to show. But a preaching-only gospel is not convincing to much of the world, nor should it be. That would be like trying to sell a car with a beautiful body but no engine.

The fact that miracles for evangelistic purposes did not remain the primary strategy for building the Church ought to give us some hope and a clue, for the Church continued to succeed without an abundance of supernatural attestation. What was its strategy? The primary power of the early Church lay not in supernaturally endued individuals, but in its corporate kingdom lifestyle.

Obviously, there are other ways to demonstrate the gospel besides corporate kingdom living. Throughout the centuries, many heroic individual deeds have been signs of the kingdom, just as testimonies of transformed lives are powerful validations of the gospel today. Parachurch ministries have done much to expand the influence of Christianity around the world. But God's primary instrument for establishing the kingdom of God is his Church, living together in love.

In a previous "Now What?" we suggested that you work on a questionnaire on the topic of the identity of Jesus to be used in conversations with non-Christians. Now it is time to demonstrate and proclaim the gospel as a group or as individuals. By the way, it is no accident that these two prongs of kingdom work relate directly to the two categories of spiritual gifts we reviewed under the quality of intensity. *Demonstrating the gospel* employs the serving gifts; *announcing the kingdom* is accomplished through the speaking gifts.

1. If you have already demonstrated your Christian testimony in your neighborhood just by being a good neighbor, take the questionnaire to one or more neighbors with whom you have a positive relationship. Tell them that you meet weekly in a small group where a discussion arose about what people in your community believe about Jesus. Mention that you are responsible to bring back a sampling of responses from your neighborhood and ask if you may ask a few questions. Proceed with the questionnaire. Do not use this meeting to evangelize, but be alert to an opening to invite further discussion.

> *Now it is time to demonstrate and proclaim the gospel as a group or as individuals.*

2. As a group, take the questionnaire to a public place such as a shopping mall or a transportation station and use the same strategy mentioned above. Work in pairs, identify your church by name so people will know you are not part of a cult, and conclude the conversation with a printed invitation to your church or some specially planned event.

3. As a group, you may enjoy working in an ongoing ministry. Here are some ways to demonstrate and proclaim the gospel:

    * Take responsibility for conducting worship services at a nursing home, making sure you spend time with the people individually.

    * Start and operate a children's club in your church, making special effort to invite non-churched children.

* Purchase, renovate and operate at low cost an inner city apartment building for disadvantaged people.

* Lead services at a rescue mission and become friends with some of the people who are being served or rehabilitated.

* If your church location is right for this, begin a commuter ministry, allowing bus or train commuters to park in the church's lot for free. Encourage them to wait inside your fellowship hall where you can offer coffee, tea, hot chocolate or cool drinks at a nominal charge, and feature a book table with good, topical Christian books, the daily newspaper, and free Christian literature.

> *Keep alert to the needs in your specific neighborhoods, and offer practical helps.*

* As a group join a local service agency: volunteer fire fighters, Jaycees, Lions Club, Rotary, Kiwanis, ambulance corps. Establish relationships for friendship evangelism.

* Purchase radio spots on a local station, and present short messages directed to men and women about their role as parents, and how the church can help them.

* On Thanksgiving or another holiday, take your families to a center in your city or town where the homeless are being fed, and share the mealtime with them.

* Keep alert to the needs in your specific neighborhoods, and offer practical helps (raking or shoveling for the elderly, bringing food to the ill, talking with the lonely).

CHAPTER NINE

PRAYING TENACIOUSLY

Disciple Quality: **DEPENDENCY**

WHAT IT SAYS

LESSON TWENTY-FIVE
Read Luke 11:1-13

Does it seem odd that the disciples of Jesus had to ask him to teach them to pray? Did they not already know how, having been raised in Jewish homes? And even more strange: why did not Jesus take the initiative? In most modern discipleship methods, one of the first lessons is the cultivation of a "quiet time," or devotions.

Here we see the disciples of Jesus, who noticed that John the Baptist's disciples prayed, as taught by their leader, coming to Jesus to ask him to do the same for them. The followers of Jesus had observed him in prayer on several occasions, or at least they saw him departing for a place of prayer (see Luke 6:12; 11:1). They must have been impressed that even their Lord, who they knew was also the Messiah, prayed with complete **dependency** upon God. The disciples knew they would need to learn to pray effectively because one time when they had failed to expel a demon from a young boy, Jesus told them, *"This kind can come out only by prayer"* (Mark 9:29).

So we should not be surprised that the disciples wanted to learn to pray. But why did Jesus not make this a priority and teach them earlier? We can only speculate, but perhaps the reason was precisely because praying is so vitally important and so difficult to maintain that Jesus waited until the disciples were inwardly motivated. No amount of external urging will prevail in getting people to live prayerfully. The amount of discipline required is very great, and the amount of faith required to persist is even greater.

> *No amount of external urging will prevail in getting people to live prayerfully.*

Now that the disciples hungered to know how to pray, Jesus gladly taught them. But notice how he did it. He did not develop a theology of prayer; he did not teach the principles of prayer. Rather, he gave them a very simple pattern for praying, which includes the basic elements: worship, intercession, petition, confession, guidance, protection, and affirmation. Luke's version of the prayer is shorter than the more familiar one found in Matthew 6, but contains all the same elements.

1. Which phrase in the Lord's Prayer reveals each of these elements?

Confession _____

Affirmation _____

Worship _____

Guidance _____

Petition _____

Intercession _____

Protection _____

> Out of an hour of praying, how many minutes do you spend on each?
>
> Do you think this is about the right balance? If not, how would you adjust it?

2. What are the differences between asking, seeking, and knocking?

> Do these suggest different kinds of praying? If so, how?

3. How does the story about the midnight request (Luke 11:5-8) illustrate our need?

> How does it illustrate God's response?

4. What does the illustration about a father and son demonstrate about prayer?

> Why might Jesus have used such dramatic imagery?

5. Can you discover three truths about the Holy Spirit that are suggested in Luke 11:1-13?

WHAT IT MEANS

LESSON TWENTY-SIX

The most unusual feature in this prayer is the direct address to God as Father (Abba). This implied a level of intimacy with the Almighty, which the Jewish leaders would not assume. While this intimacy is assumed, there is no lack of reverence. The sacredness of God is quickly affirmed, as is his kingship, thus setting the groundwork for worship and adoration, as well as petition and confession. God's transcendence and sovereignty qualify him to be worshipped, and the better we understand the greatness of these attributes, the deeper will be our worship. An anemic life of worship betrays an inadequate understanding of God. In the worship phase of the prayer we touch eternity.

The petition focuses on two basic needs, pointing to the present and the future. We beseech God to supply our daily needs, and we ask for guidance: *"give us this day. . ."* and *"lead us not."*

Dependency upon God for daily bread is an admission of his ownership of all creation and his benevolence to his creatures. It is also a denial of self-sufficiency and ingratitude. By asking for daily bread *"this day"* we are brought to these attitudes frequently, and Jesus implies that prayer is to be a daily practice.

The prayer for guidance and protection recognizes the reality of the other kingdom, the domain of the evil one who delights in putting the Father's children in places of temptation, or testing. This petition may be a request for guidance, protection, or deliverance.

Surprisingly to many of us, the prayer of confession is not uttered first. As the entire prayer proceeds from a humble and contrite heart, perhaps the order is not too important. While adoration points toward eternity, and petition focuses on the present and the future, confession looks to the past. The penitent pray-er may boldly request remission of sins because he has already extended such forgiveness to others. He is not asking God to do for him what he, the sinner, has not been willing to do for others. The acknowledgement of sins is a total repentance with the expressed desire not again to trespass or transgress.

> *While adoration points toward eternity, and petition focuses on the present and the future, confession looks to the past.*

The whole tenor of the prayer is **dependency**—depending upon God for: the basic Father / child relationship, his kingdom to reign, daily bread to be provided, forgiveness to be extended, and protection to be ensured.

6. In an affluent culture, is living dependently necessary?

   If not, how can Christians learn to live dependently upon God?

   Why is biblical **dependency** important for disciples of Jesus?

7. What is your understanding of:

   Independence

   Co-dependence

Interdependence

Dependence

Which of the above four terms best describes the most ideal relationship for the believer with:

God

Non-Christians

Christians

8. What might be the evidence that a Christian has learned to live dependently upon God?

If you know someone who fits this description, tell about him or her, and what you have observed about this person.

9. Describe the opposite of living dependently. How does this relate to the attitude of gratitude?

10. How does the "Lord's Prayer" give us an inside look into the heart of Jesus and his relationship with the Father?

WHAT IT MEANS FOR ME

LESSON TWENTY-SEVEN

The two parables in our text affirm the appropriateness of our **dependency**. The Father will respond out of his fatherly heart of generosity and love. Our **dependency** may be stretched to persistence at times; we may need to ask, and to seek, and to knock, but the heavenly Father will show himself to be better than an earthly father, who gives good gifts to his children. Our Father will give his Holy Spirit to satisfy our **dependency.** All that we require will be found in this Source.

Other scriptures indicate that he, the Holy Spirit, provides guidance, comfort, truth, encouragement, and conviction. He also gives inspiration to our prayers when we do not know what to pray (Romans 8:26). Thus, the Father has done better than giving us the occasional answer to the prayers we think to pray; he has sent permanently part of himself to reside with us.

11. Do you think Jesus meant for this prayer to be uttered daily?

If so, what might this suggest about the validity and value of disciplined daily prayer, even liturgy?

If not, what was his intention with the word "daily"?

12. Has there been a time in your life when you were keenly aware of your dependence upon God? Share that experience.

13. How has this study of the Lord's Prayer influenced your concept of God?

14. How has this study affected your understanding about prayer?

15. As you have studied this passage the past several weeks, have you grown in your **dependency**?

    If so, encourage others in the group by telling how.

    Pray for each other to grow in the area of **dependency.**

NOW WHAT?

Kingdom Strategy #9

People of the kingdom place their full confidence in the goodness and power of God, continually depending on him for provisions, forgiveness, guidance, and spiritual strength.

Here is a strange paradox: Jesus prayed. During his earthly ministry, the eternal Son of God, who lived continually with his Father in intimacy, and who possessed all the power of deity, was frequently seen to pray. If he always knew the Father's will, was always in communion with him, and could always provide whatever was needed, why did Jesus pray?

The complete answer to that question is beyond our grasp. In the mystical union of the Godhead there is much that remains incomprehensible to finite man. In a more simplistic sense, however, we do know why Jesus prayed. He wanted to. Wherever relationship runs deep, communication is precious, intimate, and inevitable. The bond between the Father and the Son made prayer the most natural and reasonable of all Jesus' activities on earth. Part of the mystery of the Trinity is that the God-man had the ability to be completely autonomous, yet he continually lived dependently in union with his Father. Our God is a loving Father who wants our relationship with him to be characterized by dependency, and the belief that he is more than adequate to meet our needs. He also wants us to be tenacious in our praying, being confident that he will answer according to his good time and will. As we grow in our life of prayer and **dependency**, we will be modeling Kingdom Strategy #9.

One effective and helpful way to use the Lord's Prayer is to let each phrase guide you in the various elements of prayer. Use "Our Father" to reaffirm your relationship with God, giving thanks for your adoption into his family and the price he paid for you. The "hallowed" phrase will lead you into worship. Ponder God's greatness, his majesty, his awesomeness. Revere and adore him. Maybe praying a Psalm to him will help you. Some excellent ones for this purpose are: 8, 23, 29, 33, 93, 96, 103, 111, 139, and 145.

> *Ponder God's greatness, his majesty, his awesomeness. Revere and adore him.*

The prayer for God's kingdom to come may guide you into intercession for the world. Missions, political injustices, social and criminal evils, and the triumph of the church may be some appropriate themes. Also express your longing for the return of Jesus.

The prayer for daily bread moves you to personal concerns. All provisions for life and ministry may be requested here. Food, clothing, shelter, and health are basic needs. Having the ability to meet other financial commitments and to contribute to God's work is also prayer that fit this petition section. This part of the praying will embrace the needs of your family and anyone who looks to you for support.

Confession is the next feature in the Lord's Prayer. Spend time examining your life and attitudes. The "General Confession" in *The Book of Common Prayer* suggests in generalities the ways we sin:

> *Almighty and most merciful Father; We have erred and strayed from thy ways, like lost sheep. We have followed too much the devices and desires of our own hearts. We have offended against thy holy laws. We have left undone those things which we ought to have done; And we have done those things which we ought not to have done; And there is no health in us.*[vii]

But do not settle for these generalities. As God brings to your mind specific sins, confess them. Be aware especially of attitudes, the inward sins which only you may know about, but which hinder your walk with the Lord and your fruitfulness in ministry.

After confessing, ask for forgiveness. The second part of the "General Confession" conveys the spirit of seeking forgiveness:

> *But thou, O Lord, have mercy upon us, miserable offenders. Spare thou those, O God, who confess their faults. Restore thou those who are penitent; According to thy promises declared unto mankind in Christ Jesus our Lord. And grant, O most merciful Father, for his sake; that we may hereafter live a godly, righteous, and sober life, To the glory of thy holy Name. Amen.*[viii]

Realize that God expects you to extend the same grace of forgiveness to others. Are there people who have sinned against you? Are you willing to forgive them? Have you forgiven them? Declare these thoughts to God as you pray the section *"As we forgive those who have trespassed against us."*

Lastly, pray for guidance and protection. Acknowledge your proneness to fall into sin. Tell God about the trials and testings you are facing. Ask him to spare you from trials which are unnecessary for your character development. As trials come, trust that God has allowed them for your growth, and ask him to deliver you through them. More positively, ask him to lead you into productive ministry during that day.

Pray this way each day for a week. Then consider whether your sense of dependency upon God has increased. Be willing to share your experience with others in the group. Continue this practice as God leads.

CHAPTER TEN

SPEAKING HONESTLY

Disciple Quality: **TRANSPARENCY**

WHAT IT SAYS

LESSON TWENTY-EIGHT
Read Luke 12:1-12

Christians often hear the adage, "Walk your talk," an admonition to live consistently with what we say we believe. That is a fine goal, but it assumes that our talk is godly. Most of us know better than that; our talk is often not worthy to direct our walk. The apostle James was convinced that the human tongue is the source of most sin, and if a person could control his tongue, he or she would be a perfect person (James 3:2).

Why is our speech so important? Is it not because truth and love are the supreme virtues, and our talk is a primary way to communicate both truth and love? The Gospels present Jesus as a very tolerant person, able to see beneath the exterior of a person's life to their interior, and respond, not on the basis of the outward sins of a person's life, but on the potential of their true person, the inward man. Sometimes, however, when Jesus looked on the inside, what he saw was ugly. In those cases he did not fail to confront the problem.

> *Our talk is often not worthy to direct our walk.*

The text for this unit of lessons begins with a warning to the disciples about respectable exterior but ugly interior. Rather than covering up their true selves, Jesus encouraged **transparency.** He used the Pharisees as an example of what not to be like. In the previous chapter, Luke 11, we see why Jesus warned his followers about the Pharisees. In eleven verses, Luke 11:42-52, Jesus pronounced six "Woes" upon the Pharisees. It might be helpful to look up this passage and see what Jesus was condemning.

Notice that Jesus attacked their:

- Hypocrisy – emphasis on insignificant rules (v.42)
- Pride – desire for recognition (v.43)
- Corruption – covered by a spotless exterior (v.44)

- Elitism – imposing impossible standards on others (v.46)
- Murderous disposition (v.47)
- False teaching (v.52)

Lack of truth and lack of love are at the root of all six of these sins. Fullness of truth and love are seen in the way Jesus spoke to the issues. Notice that Jesus was not gossiping behind the backs of the Pharisees. He spoke to them directly; in each case he said, *"Woe to you."* So when we get to Luke 12 and hear Jesus warning his disciples about the Pharisees, we have already seen his example of honest confrontation. Jesus would not say about the Pharisees anything he had not already said to them.

How often in the church we abuse this principle and lack **transparency**. For the sake of truth, we freely condemn others as we speak to brothers and sisters whom we know will agree with us, and we do so without first being honest and lovingly confrontational with those we are condemning.

1. Read Luke 11:53-54; why are these verses such an important context for understanding Luke 12:1-12?

2. What do you know about yeast (leaven), and why did Jesus use it as a metaphor about the Pharisees?

3. In verses 2 and 3 who do you think are the speakers and who are the disclosers?

    ____ God will disclose what everyone says

    ____ The Pharisees will disclose what the disciples say

    ____ God will disclose what the disciples say

    ____ The disciples will disclose what the Pharisees say

4. Why will such disclosure occur?

    What is the role of hypocrisy in this disclosure?

5. What was Jesus saying in verses 4 and 5 about fear?

    If any Pharisees heard this, what might they have thought?

    How can these verses help us in being faithful witnesses for Christ?

WHAT IT MEANS

LESSON TWENTY-NINE

People like to believe that even the most reprehensible person has a spark of goodness hidden inside. To the extent that we are all created in the image of God, that is true, but scripture teaches that despite the appearances of even the best of people, we are all born as sinners. Deep in our core, we are rebels against God and his ways.

Some have argued that one of the marks of real evil in a person is the desire to appear blameless, when we know we are not. A lot of energy is devoted to maintaining a veneer of respectability rather than **transparency**. Tragically, members of religious communities often exhibit precisely this same preoccupation with *appearances*, rather than reality. The Bible warns that Satan himself masquerades as an angel of light—as a being who looks good, while, in reality, is the embodiment of evil.

From our own experience, each of us can probably admit to having engaged in cover-ups; in some way or other, at some time or other, we have presented a false front. Fear and pride, separately or together, are at the root of this cover-up. Concern that others may reject me (fear), or a desire to advance myself (pride) may lead me to ensure that others see me as "good." This preference may cause me to create or maintain that impression even if—and here comes the hypocrisy—I know their perception is false.

6. What does it mean to be transparent?

    Why is **transparency** so important for doing kingdom ministry?

    What is the biblical term closest to this concept?

7. When is **transparency** most difficult?

    Can one be too transparent? What is the relationship between **transparency** and tact?

    Can you share an event in your life when you either failed or succeeded when you were tempted to not be transparent?

8. Why is hypocrisy (v.1) a problem especially among religious people?

    What is the opposite of hypocrisy?

9. How was Jesus a victim to the truth in verses 2 and 3?

WHAT IT MEANS FOR ME

LESSON THIRTY

The motive of Jesus in the warning he gave in Luke 12:1-12 was not primarily to expose the Pharisees; rather, Jesus was concerned that his followers should not be intimidated by these so-called religious leaders. Jesus knew that the fanatical fundamentalism of the Pharisees, who long ago had accepted a creed that went far beyond Old Testament teaching into extreme legalism, would pose the most dangerous threat to the faithfulness of his disciples.

In first century Judaism the Pharisees were the fundamentalists; the Sadducees were a far more liberal party and were not much of a threat to Jesus. Primarily, it was the Pharisees who incited hatred toward Jesus, and who by their lies, deception, and political slimery instigated the trial and crucifixion of Jesus.

In the face of conservative religious pressure, the temptation to renounce our convictions and go along with the prevailing mood is very great. Most Christians more easily stand firm in the face of liberal opposition. Jesus wanted to make sure his followers knew that they would be tested by the extreme right, and in the face of that pressure they should not back away from the truth out of fear. Betraying honesty should not be the price for acceptance by the religious community.

> *Although faithfulness to truth may demand a great price, compromising the truth demands an even greater price.*

Jesus was not teaching his disciples that "honesty is the best policy" for personal gain, but that although faithfulness to truth may demand a great price, compromising the truth demands an even greater price. The truthful Christian may lose his life, as Jesus did, but the unfaithful one will be disowned *"before the angels of God."* If denial of one's faith goes as far as blaspheming the Holy Spirit, that sin will not be forgiven.

10. Can you think of situations in which you knowingly allow (or even create) an impression that stretches or distorts the truth about yourself? Looking into your heart, do you detect fear or pride (or both) at the root?

11. What can you do to correct the situation now, or to preclude such a situation from arising in the future? Can the members of your discipleship group help?

12. Notice the six "Woes" in Luke 11 (listed in Lesson Twenty-eight). Toward which of these hypocrisies are you most prone?

13. Have you ever been betrayed by someone who disclosed something confidential? Tell about it.

    Discuss the importance of preserving the confidentiality of things discussed in your discipleship group.

14. Discuss the level of **transparency** you have within your group.

   Is there enough self-revealing to be accountable to one another?

   What would it take for there to be greater **transparency**?

   Pray for each other to grow in the area of **transparency.**

NOW WHAT?

Kingdom Strategy #10

Because disciples believe that the kingdom of God is the realm where truth prevails, they strive to have honest and open relationships.

One of the worldly tendencies toward which men are particularly prone is artificiality. We try to project a culturally defined image instead of revealing God's workmanship—our real, humble self as it is transformed in Christ. Men call this being "macho." A real man, we've been told, is aggressive and invulnerable and has no soft, "feminine" feelings. Emotions are for women, we say. We wear a "tough guy" mask, call it masculinity, and preserve our shallowness and superficiality. In reality, such hiding is blatant cowardice that keeps us from becoming involved with others and their weaknesses under the pretense that we ourselves are strong.

For some reason, appearing to be self-sufficient is very important to most men. Much of our so-called masculinity is tied to the idea of strength, physical and otherwise. Any sign of weakness is seen as undermining our manhood. This is one reason why religion is far more popular with women than with men. Religion implies a sense of need, an ability to own up to our weakness and dependency. It requires petition, adoration, humility, caring, and other expressions of emotion that seem threatening to many men because they expose our weaknesses. Most Christian men have much to learn about true strength, the willingness to appear as we really are, secure in the knowledge that who we are in Christ is adequate.

The **transparency** we have been considering is a special kind of truthfulness; it might be called full-disclosure truthfulness. Some people are truthful, but they are very private and opaque. They do not self-reveal enough to help others or themselves.

Consider the quote below. Meditate on it. Examine yourself by it.

In this questioning of truthfulness, what matters first and last is that a man's whole being should be exposed, his whole evil laid bare in the sight of God. But sinful men do not like this sort of truthfulness, and they resist it with all their might. That is why they persecute it and crucify it. It is only because we follow Jesus that we can be genuinely truthful, for then he reveals to us our sin upon the Cross. The Cross is God's truth about us, and therefore it is the only power which can make us truthful. When we know the Cross we are no longer afraid of the truth. We need no more oaths to confirm the truth of our utterances, for we live in the perfect truth of God.

There is no truth toward Jesus without truth toward man. Untruthfulness destroys fellowship, but truth cuts false fellowship to pieces and establishes genuine brotherhood. We cannot follow Christ unless we live in revealed truth before God and man.

From *The Cost of Discipleship* by Dietrich Bonhoeffer[ix]

CHAPTER ELEVEN

LIVING CARE FREE

Disciple Quality: **CONTENTMENT**

WHAT IT SAYS

LESSON THIRTY-ONE
Read Luke 12:22-34

From what do you get your sense of well-being or **contentment**? Most of us have a number of foundations on which we build our sense of well-being. Sadly, nearly all of these foundations are inadequate.

From what do you get your sense of **contentment**? One way to discover your answer is to look for the things you worry about. In Luke 12:22-34 Jesus identified food, clothes, and possessions as the common items which worry us.

Secondly, to discover your foundations for security, reflect on the characteristics about which you compare yourself with others. Your appearance? Education? Social standing? The Apostle Paul disapproved the tendency to compare ourselves with others. He wrote about it so frequently (see, for example, Phil. 2:2-3; 2 Cor. 5:16; Rom. 12:3) that we must conclude that he saw comparing as a common practice. Each of us can confirm this from our own practice.

A third way to find the truth here is to look at the things you boast about. Even though boasting is not acceptable behavior, we all know what it is to drop subtle hints about a subject in which we take pride. We all boast, even if only in the privacy of our hearts. We all have thoughts of pride.

1. In Luke 12:22-34 what does Jesus say about food? The future? Clothing?

    What do these thoughts suggest about wealth?

2. How do the truths about ravens, lilies, and grass (verses 24, 27, and 28) reduce us to level living with others?

3. Notice all the references to worry and anxiety in Luke 12:22-34. Although we may not worry about food and clothes literally, what might they symbolize in your life?

   What are evidences of worry?

   Why are we not to worry?

4. What are the thieves and moths (verse 33) in our day?

   What do they threaten that are precious to you?

5. What do you learn in this passage about treasure?

   What of your possessions do you protect most vigorously?

   What is "treasure in heaven"?

WHAT IT MEANS

LESSON THIRTY-TWO

Jubilee living (see Leviticus 25) challenges us to eliminate all the false foundations, all the useless worries, all the pretensions to greatness or personal merit. The disciplines required for a weekly day of rest, the Sabbath year, and above all, Jubilee Year were intended to restore the rightful economic and social order in the world. More importantly, these disciplines sought to restore men and women to rightful relationships with God, relationships which find security in him.

> *Jubilee living challenges us to eliminate all the false foundations, all the useless worries, all the pretensions to greatness or personal merit.*

The notion of finding our security in God strikes at the heart of our natural, worldly tendency to depend on personal accomplishments or characteristics. In particular, we depend upon:

- Material wealth
- Life circumstances
- Personal righteousness

6. How is *"life more than food, and the body more than clothes"*?

   Why would Jesus need to say this?

7. What is the difference between owning and possessing?

   Why is **contentment** an important quality for disciples in ministry?

   How might you determine whether you own your possessions or they own you?

8. What does *"seek his kingdom"* mean?

   What would seeking his kingdom do specifically to change your lifestyle?

9. Why do you think Jesus referred to his disciples as *"men of little faith"* (verse 28) and a *"little flock"* (verse 32)?

   How is the adjective "little" usually perceived?

10. In what aspects of life have you been particularly fortunate—where you are certainly not little?

    Do you either take pride or occasionally look down on others who seem inferior to you in these areas?

Pray together, asking forgiveness for the specific ways you may have misused material wealth or your attitudes about material things. Seek the Lord's guidance in identifying practical steps you can take to apply the Jubilee principles in your daily handling of material wealth.

WHAT IT MEANS FOR ME

LESSON THIRTY-THREE

Jesus' words in Luke 12 strike right at the heart of the world's wrong understanding of value. Taken seriously, his teaching points out the uneasy truth that investing in material assets to accumulate "net worth" is, ultimately, worthless. Any notion that I have my wealth to use and manage (plan, control) for whatever goals I wish is based on the illusion that my life, too, is Mine!

> *But God said to him, "You fool! This very night your life will be demanded of you. Then who will get what you have prepared for yourself?"* (Luke 12:20)

In our society, nevertheless, we often attach inordinate significance to a person's ability to pile up a large nest egg. When a person dies, we often hear, "How much was he worth?", as if to suggest that the total worth of the deceased was what he possessed. We also hear, "How much did he leave behind?" Of course, the correct answer always is, "All of it." Jesus words in Luke 12:33-34 suggest a different type of nest egg.

Sell your possessions and give to the poor. Provide purses for yourselves that will not wear out, a treasure in heaven that will not be exhausted, where no thief comes near and no moth destroys. For where your treasure is, there your heart will be also.

11. In Luke 12:33 Jesus told his disciples to sell their possessions and give the money to charity. How would you have felt if he asked you to do this?

    To what extent does Jesus require us literally to give away everything?

    What would have to happen to reduce or eliminate your dependency on material wealth?

12. If one of your close friends were asked to say what your life consists of, that is, what is most basic to who you are, what might he say?

13. The Jubilee concept teaches that we don't really own anything—that we are custodians for a time of some things entrusted to us. What are some actions you could take to use your wealth more to the glory of God?

    As a manager for the Master, how frequently do you ask the Lord how he wants his assets invested?

14. Who are some of the people (or groups) you pull away from?

    What part do external symbols of success (abundance of food and fashion) play in setting you (or them) apart?

15. Jubilee living forbids us to hold others in our power. How might the people (or groups) you listed above perceive you to be holding power over them?

    What do you need to do to release them? Will you do it?

16. What impact have these lessons on security had upon your life?

Pray with one another, asking not only for forgiveness for any sense of superiority, but also for the strength to act in ways that demonstrate level living—our common, shared standing before God.
Pray for each other to grow in the area of **contentment.**

NOW WHAT?

Kingdom Strategy #11

Sabbath and Jubilee principles, with their economic, social, and theological implications, must govern a disciple's everyday lifestyle.

Jesus was a poor man according to earthly standards. He was born into abject poverty in a stable, spent most of his time with the poorer social class, and died possessing only the garments he wore. But imagine what he might have accrued during his days on earth! How much would Jairus the synagogue official been willing to pay for his daughter to be brought back to life? How much could Jesus have charged the centurion for healing his servant? How much could Jesus have charged the hungry people for the multiplied loaves and fish? How often could he have sent Peter to the sea to pull up a fish with a coin in its mouth or filled his nets with fish? How much could he have charged the ten lepers for healing them?

Such questions could go on and on, citing all the ways Jesus ministered sensationally to others. But Jesus never cashed in on his power. In fact, he taught that poverty is a blessing when it enriches spirituality. We know that Jesus did not proclaim Jubilee Year (see Leviticus 25) for kingdom living merely to abolish poverty by redistributing tangible goods. Rather, Jesus wanted others to see the principles of God's kingdom expressed in his followers. Disciples are honorable contented people who know how to forgive debts and live carefree, trusting in God's provisions. They do not use money as an instrument of power, because they understand that all material resources belong to a loving God who has sovereignty regarding their investment. Being liberated from our own materialistic concerns allows us to concentrate on the well being of others, which is the point of Kingdom Strategy #11.

Imagine that your house is on fire and you have only three minutes to save your most valuable possessions. How would you use those three minutes? In the space provided below, list in any order the items (not people; we'll assume they are all safe) you would try to save. Be as realistic and honest in your selection as you can. You might list: financial records, wedding album, jewelry, heirloom, TV, etc.

Now rate them in order of priority, putting a 1 beside the article that means most to you, a 2 by the one that comes next, etc. Now think about the items you have rated 1, 2, and 3. Why are they valuable to you? Sentimental, financial, professional, spiritual, social reasons? Jot down your reason beside those three most important items.

Item	Priority	Reason

In your group take turns sharing the items you saved, explaining why in each case. Make sure everyone understands it is not presumed wrong to want to salvage material things. Then, however, have an open discussion about how you'd feel if you were literally asked to give away these possessions. Reconsider question 11 in Lesson Thirty-three, and review your main source of security.

REVIEW

"Learning Kingdom Ministry" was the middle component in the training of the disciples. The first module, found in chapter five and six of Luke, and chapters 1-5 in *"Follow Me"*, focused on the character qualities that would enable the disciples to move with Jesus into ministry. As they followed him, they were astonished both by the things he said and the authority he demonstrated as he healed people and performed other miracles.

While Jesus wanted them to gain the maturity that would be needed for kingdom ministry, he continued to teach them the discipleship qualities they would need to re-present him. The six qualities we have just studied are needed for effectiveness out in the world.

Before moving into the final module of Luke's presentation of the training of the twelve, it is timely to take stock of our progress. As individuals, and then as a group, review the preceeding six chapters and discuss the examples of Jesus and your own progress in each area.

Discipleship Quality	Example from Jesus	My Progress
Selflessness		
Intensity		
Courage		
Dependency		
Transparency		
Contentment		

UNIT THREE

LEARNING KINGDOM LEADERSHIP
Being a Disciple in the Church

Trustworthiness	*Accountability*
Alertness	*Servanthood*

CHAPTER TWELVE

MANAGING WISELY

Disciple Quality: **TRUSTWORTHINESS**

WHAT IT SAYS

LESSON THIRTY-FOUR
Read Luke 16:1-13

Christians and non-Christians alike have for centuries admired the teaching ability of Jesus. Both his message and his methodology were the stuff of true genius. As a teacher, Jesus employed a variety of techniques to impress his message upon his hearers, but perhaps his use of parables is what comes most quickly to mind when people think about the teaching of Jesus. He drew readily from the common, everyday experiences of life to communicate the most important truths any teacher has ever delivered.

Most of the parables work by analogy, that is, it is possible through the story or metaphor to understand the intended point by grasping a similar, perhaps more immediate idea. For example, a very valuable pearl, which a merchant would sell all his other possessions to obtain, expresses clearly the value of the kingdom of God, which is worth the sacrifice of everything (Matt. 13:45-46).

But not all parables work quite that way. Luke contains three parables that can be understood only if one looks for contrast rather than similarity. The parable Jesus used to teach his disciples about **trustworthiness** is such a parable. In this case, despite the dishonesty of the main character, he is *wise* in his concern to establish lasting relationships with other people.

Crucial to understanding this parable is seeing its context in Luke and in the ministry of Jesus. It is the fourth of five parables strung together, but it is different from the other four, which were spoken for the benefit of a public audience, primarily the Pharisees. This parable was specifically told to the disciples.

> *The cunning of the unrighteous steward was used to show that even people of this world are resourceful in preserving relationships.*

1. In the parable of the shrewd manager (Luke 16:1-13) what are some of the stated and unstated contrasts?

2. The setting for this parable, as well as the three parables in chapter 15, seems to be given in Luke 15:1-2. How does knowing this context impact your understanding of the parable?

3. How does the parable illustrate the saying in:

    - Verse 10?

    - Verse 11?

    - Verse 12?

4. To what might the following phrases refer?

    - *people of the light* v.8

    - *eternal dwellings* v.9

    - *true riches* v.11

WHAT IT MEANS

LESSON THIRTY-FIVE

The parable of "the clever rascal," as T.W. Manson calls this story, was a lesson to the disciples about the value of relationships. The cunning of the unrighteous steward was used not to commend deceitful business practices, but to show that even people of this world are resourceful in preserving relationships. It is not the method of preserving those relationships that is the point; it is the high priority placed on them, even when the gain would be temporary. Jesus was commending **trustworthiness,** and in particular, Christian savvy.

The lesson was this: just as people of the world have the savvy to employ relationships to their own advantage, so should disciples of the kingdom have the savvy or shrewdness to foster relationships that will accrue to the advantage of the eternal world.

An example of one who was not spiritually shrewd is given in the next parable. The rich man, who "lived in luxury every day" and ignored the poor beggar Lazarus, found himself in the next life in torment in hell, asking only to have his tongue cooled by a drop of water brought by Lazarus, who was now comfortably resting in Abraham's company. The rich man would have done well to have heeded the advice of verse 9, *I tell you, use worldly wealth to gain friends for yourselves, so that when it is gone, you will be welcomed into eternal dwellings.*

5. If you had been one of the twelve disciples to whom this parable was addressed, how do you think you would have understood it?

6. We are using the words *trustworthiness, spiritual shrewdness and Christian savvy* synonymously in this lesson. What does each of these concepts suggest to you?

   In your opinion, which of these terms best fits the main character of the parable?

   Which one best fits you?

7. How is it possible to detect **trustworthiness**?

   How is it possible to develop **trustworthiness**?

   Why is **trustworthiness** critical for kingdom leadership?

8. Why would the master praise the unrighteous steward, especially after relieving him of his job?

9. Do you believe management of property or assets is a spiritual activity? Why or why not?

WHAT IT MEANS FOR ME

LESSON THIRTY-SIX

This chapter has much in common with chapter four, "Responding To Rejection." Frequently the relationships that we do not maintain are with those where we are rejected or where we reject someone. Go back to question 12 in Lesson Twelve and review your progress with these people. Have these relationships improved? If not, why not?

The force of this chapter is not so much on being rejected as it is on not rejecting others. Usually to justify breaking relationships we lay most of the fault on the other party. There may be times when a relationship must be broken, but the more mature we are in our faith, the less likely or less frequently such ruptures will occur. Sometimes believers smugly take the injunction, *Come out from their midst and be separate, says the Lord* (2 Corinthians 6:17), as an excuse to avoid or break relationships with unbelievers. Paul's use of this Old Testament paraphrase was meant to tell the Corinthian disciples not to participate in pagan festivals with unbelievers. Interestingly, the word *separate* is the meaning of Pharisee. If disciples of Jesus are to be like salt and light that penetrate the world (Matthew 5:13, 14), they must be involved with unbelievers and achieve good relationships.

Jesus made it clear in his "high priestly prayer" that he expected his followers to function well in the world (John 17:15-18). In fact, he was sending them into the world. Their **trustworthiness** would be assured as they were sanctified, that is, set apart, not from the world, but set apart unto God for the sacred mission of representing him in the world.

10. Why would Jesus be particularly concerned about the stewardship of relationships?

11. Name and tell about a person who exemplifies the qualities below, and tell why you believe that about him or her:

    - Good stewardship of relationships

    - Shrewd management of spiritual resources

12. Christian children may be isolated from, immersed in, or insulated from the world. How do you evaluate each of these possibilities, and how do/did/will you as a parent seek the best balance?

13. Tell about any Christian you know whom non-Christians actually enjoy. What makes him or her like this?

14. Think of a relationship with a Christian or non-Christian that you have "squandered." Name the person:

    How might greater patience or love on your part have preserved this relationship?

    Is there a way you can restore the relationship?

    How?

    Will you?

    Pray for each other to grow in the area of **trustworthiness.**

NOW WHAT?

Kingdom Strategy # 12

Disciples of the kingdom practice spiritual shrewdness, which reflects the faithful and wise stewardship of all resources, especially human relationships.

The lesson of this parable is that just as people of this world have the craftiness to employ relationships to their own advantage, so should disciples of the kingdom have the savvy, or spiritual shrewdness, to foster relationships that will accrue to the advantage of the eternal world.

Because being worldly wise is not sinful it follows that being naive about the ways of business, finance, psychology, sociology, and modern technology is not intrinsically spiritual. To establish rapport with people who desperately need to know about the eternal world, we need to show an interest in them and learn about their present circumstances. Jesus told his followers to be *"as shrewd as snakes and as innocent as doves"* (Matt. 10:16). Most Christians I know are strong on the innocent, but weak on the shrewd. Too often we Christians needlessly turn off unbelievers by our overblown piety. Even when we don't make enemies in the secular world because of our zeal for Christ, we are pitied because of our social clumsiness and our general lack of *savoir-faire*. I'm convinced that many Christians avoid cocktail parties and other "worldly" events" not because of religious scruples as much as because of the fear of being embarrassed by their inexperience with social protocol and "small talk."

Can you imagine Jesus saying, "We'll never get these tax collectors and prostitutes to the synagogue, so I guess we cannot reach them?" Being stewards of relationships means moving out of our comfort zones to mix freely with unbelievers. Being welcomed among sinners is not necessarily proof of spiritual maturity, but surely it is significant when it occurs *for Jesus' sake*. God's people should be alert and congenial, interested in their surroundings, and involved in human issues.

This exercise will take some courage and should be done only if the trust level in your group is very high. If anyone in the group thinks it best not to do this exercise, postpone it until you have consensus.

Review the description of "In," "Not In," "Of," and "Not Of," given in chapter 12 of *"Follow Me": The Disciple-making Strategy of Jesus. Now* look at the graph below which illustrates the various possibilities of involvement or withdrawal from the world. Line A represents a Christian who has removed himself from nearly all involvement in the world. Line B represents a Christian who is still strongly of the world. The ideal is line C where one is well balanced being In and Not Of the world.

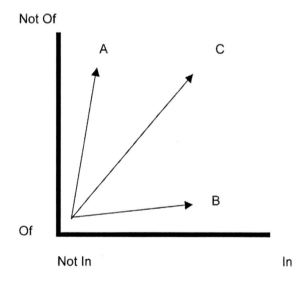

Draw another line to represent how you believe your Christian life has progressed in this issue; put your initials on the line. Now draw lines representing how you perceive each of the other people in the group has progressed. Put their initials on their lines and then share your findings with each other. Be honest; speak the truth in love. Don't be afraid to represent yourself as being closer or less close to the ideal than others are. Ultimately, where one is at the moment is not nearly as

> *Ultimately, where one is at the moment is not nearly as important as which direction one is moving.*

important as which direction one is moving. Discuss ways you can help one another move toward that Christ-like balance of line C.

Illustrate each of these possible relations of the Christian to the world:

- In but not of

- Of but not in

- Neither in nor of

- In and of

Noting where you see yourself predominantly in terms of the in/of possibilities mentioned above, discuss these questions:

1) Where is the worst point on the graph?

2) What course do new Christians usually take?

3) What are the dangers of line C?

4) What are the liabilities of line A? Of line B? Of no line?

CHAPTER THIRTEEN

CONFRONTING SIN

Disciple Quality: **ACCOUNTABILITY**

WHAT IT SAYS

LESSON THIRTY-SEVEN
Read Luke 17:1-10

We come now to a character quality which has rightfully become a very popular word in discipleship circles: **accountability.** The last third of the 20th century and the beginning of the 21st have been such a stormy era in American history that in nearly all spheres of life people have been searching for stability. Scandals in business and government have led to new standards of **accountability,** as the public demands closer scrutiny. This is also true in the church. Scandals among religious leaders have sensitized us to the importance of **accountability** for everyone.

Small group ministries provide excellent settings for **accountability.** Dr. Howard Hendricks, a well-known seminary professor, has said, "A man who is not in a group with other men is an accident waiting to happen."[x]

By this time, your group members have established deep relationships, which enable **accountability** to thrive. While being accountable is not the entire wheel of discipleship, it may be the hub. Certainly Jesus held his disciples accountable. We all need that gentle but firm discipline that holds us accountable to our convictions and commitments. Spiritual leadership, when it is exercised properly, will be like the proverbial iron fist in a velvet glove.

> *"A man who is not in a group with other men is an accident waiting to happen."*

1. Luke 17:1-10 seems to have three themes: sin, faith, and service. Notice those three sections, and discuss what the relationship might be between these themes.

2. What does *repent* mean?

    Does verse 3 say we are not to forgive unless the one who has sinned repents?

    What do other scriptures teach about this?

3. What does *forgive* mean?

    What does the Lord's Prayer teach about forgiveness?

    Are you aware of any person you have not forgiven? Who?

4. Have someone in the group read pages 212-214 from *"Follow Me": The Disciple-making Strategy of Jesus* about the relationship between millstone and the sea (v.2) and mulberry tree and the sea (v.6). What is the "root" of the problem?

    How does this relate to verse 1, "Things that cause people to sin?"

WHAT IT MEANS

LESSON THIRTY-EIGHT

In the passage before us, Luke 17:1-10, Jesus gave two commands which imply relationships of **accountability.** He told his disciples to rebuke and to forgive one another. Both of these actions are very difficult to do. Most people do not like conflict, and most of us shy away from direct confrontation. We'd rather allow a relationship to deteriorate than to get into an argument. We go by the adage, "Time heals all wounds." That might be true about wounds, but fractured relationships are not wounds; they are more like cancer, and time does not heal cancer. We find it equally difficult to forgive others. The words may come easily, but to truly forgive without holding any resentment or any sense of moral superiority—that's tough.

> *Rebuking is like using the scalpel to make an incision. Forgiving is like sewing up the incision to let it heal.*

Rebuking and forgiving are like two aspects of surgery. Rebuking is like using the scalpel to make an incision. Forgiving is like sewing up the incision to let it heal. Imagine a doctor who left all of his patients with open incisions; that's like a Christian who only rebukes and never seeks to restore relationships. Imagine a doctor who only sutures, never performing surgery because she does not like making incisions. She sews without really getting beneath the skin to the real problem. Many Christians gloss over sin and fail to confront it. Both rebuking and forgiving are essential in spiritual surgery.

The activity in between the incision and the suturing—the real reason for the surgery—is called repentance. Rebuking does not eradicate sin, and forgiving does not either, any more than an incision and suturing make a successful operation. The work in between is most important. Rebuking just enables us to get at the problem. Forgiving just enables healing to occur after the problem has been treated. Repentance is the most important part. Notice how repentance stands right in the middle:

> *If your brother sins, <u>rebuke</u> him, and if he <u>repents</u>, <u>forgive</u> him.*
>
> Luke 17:3, emphasis added

5. Who are the *"little ones"* referred to in verse 2?

   How are they sometimes caused to sin?

6. What is implied in Jesus' admonition *"So watch yourselves"* in verse 3?

   How can believers best watch themselves?

7. Why did the disciples ask for greater faith?

   What does Jesus' answer teach us about faith?

8. "You" in verse 6 is plural; how does this affect the interpretation of this verse?

   Should rebuking, repenting, and forgiving be private or public? What principle should guide our decision about this?

9. What do verses 7-10 have to do with **accountability**? Why did Jesus tell this parable?

   Why is **accountability** so important for leaders in the kingdom?

10. What does it mean to rebuke someone?

    Without violating privacy, share an experience when you rebuked someone, or when you were rebuked. In light of Galatians 6:1, was it done properly?

    Has rebuking ever occurred in your group? If not, are you holding one another accountable?

WHAT IT MEANS FOR ME

LESSON THIRTY-NINE

In the Old Testament **accountability** was summed up in the word *covenant*. The covenant between God and his people was intended to help them live by the lifestyle and hold to the beliefs which God had instructed. Even though we do not as frequently use the word *covenant* today, the same dynamic should be in place in the Christian family and the church. God's community is expected to live faithfully to his teachings, and we are to "police" ourselves. That is why he has established leaders; that is why he admonishes us to remain in fellowship with one another.

There are two more important things to notice about biblical **accountability**: first, **accountability** is between brothers or sisters, that is, between Christians. The relationship must be repaired so the family can remain intact. Also, the rebuking is done to confront sin. We are not given license to rebuke others for their annoying habits, for their accidental failures, or for inconveniencing us. The issue is sin. And about sin, disciples must become much more serious, both for the sake of the family of God and for the sake of the sinner who needs to be restored.

As seen above, Galatians 6:1 gives a helpful approach to spiritual **accountability**:

> *Brothers, if a man is trapped in some sin, you who are spiritual should restore him gently. But watch yourself; you also may be tempted.*

11. Why is the master's expectation in verse 8 not unreasonable?

    Why did Jesus in verse 10 compare this expectation with obedience by the disciples?

    What is the *duty* Jesus was talking about in verse 10?

12. In what areas of life do men and women need to be held accountable?

    What are some practical ways people can hold each other accountable?

13. Personalize this issue now. What sin(s) are holding back your spiritual growth?

    If you are not being accountable to anyone about this sin, are you willing to be?

    To whom in your group would it be best for you to be accountable?

14. Let's not fool ourselves. We know the real issues. John spelled them out quite clearly: the lusts of the flesh, the lusts of the eyes, and the pride of life (1 John 2:16). Money, sex, and power are the words Richard Foster[xi] uses to describe these temptations in his book *Money, Sex and Power*. John helps us be honest by saying we, as believers, all sin. Read 1 John 1:8-10.

This exercise may be difficult for you, but we are at cutting edge discipleship right now. As honest as you can be, finish the sentences below.

My greatest problem in the money area of my life is:

My greatest problem in the sex area of my life is:

My greatest problem in the power area of my life is:

Of the three above, the one that troubles me most is:

The type of occasion when this is most likely to surface as a temptation is:

15. Make a covenant with one another that the issues shared in this session (as should be the case always) will never be mentioned in any other setting to any other person. Arrange to meet during the week with your "Accountability Buddy" for further sharing and prayer. This may mean two meetings, one in which you are the "accounter" and one in which you are the "accountee."

Pray for each other to grow in the area of **accountability.**

NOW WHAT?

Kingdom Strategy #13

Disciples must become accountable, which entails confronting sin in each other courageously and compassionately for the purpose of stimulating each others' spiritual advancement.

Jesus knew that the human tendency to undermine the spiritual standards of others existed even in his followers, so he gave them a very serious warning about the consequences of inhibiting others from making spiritual progress. Christian disciples enjoy great liberty, especially when compared to the legalistic Pharisees, but such freedom can easily develop into a license in ethical standards that may be especially harmful to less mature believers. The liberty that Jesus modeled for his followers must be used prudently, which is why he told them to "watch" themselves.

In the 1980's the evangelical church in America was suddenly hit by repeated scandals involving Christian celebrities. All the drama normally associated with afternoon soap operas could be seen on the nightly news as several famous Christians "fell" to financial fraud, adultery, pornography, and assorted other sins. The church, which had enjoyed "the Decade of the Evangelicals," was now being ridiculed by the world. It was like finding a Puritan in a brothel. In shame, we Christians found ourselves awkwardly explaining to the general public that each scandal was a rare exception. But then another one would hit the headlines.

Sadly, these leaders had neglected a very fundamental Christian dynamic: **accountability**. No doubt each one agreed with the theological concept of unity in the body of Christ, which presupposes **accountability**, but the theology was not translated into life.

Earlier we said that perhaps **accountability** is the hub of the wheel of discipleship. You might think that we should have discussed it first, or at least a lot earlier. We have been following Luke's order, and so we notice that Jesus waited quite a while before raising this issue with his disciples.

> *Accountability—and especially rebuking and forgiving—demands very deep relationships.*

Accountability—and especially rebuking and forgiving—demands very deep relationships. The trust level between believers must be very secure before **accountability** will really occur.

No doubt the most difficult aspect of **accountability** is the embarrassment each of us feels as we reveal our areas of weakness. The tendency will be to avoid outright sins of commission and focus on sins of omission. "I need more discipline in my devotional life," or "I need to spend more time with the kids," or "I really should lose some weight and exercise more"—these may be true, but probably are not at the cutting edge of growth for you. They may be smoke screens to avoid having to come clean with the real issues in your life.

Having gone through the rather painful exercises of questions 13 and 14, if anyone in the group thinks as a group you have not addressed the most important issues by your answers there, go over that question again (repeated below):

Personalize this issue now. What sin(s) are holding back your spiritual growth?

If you are not being accountable to anyone about this sin, are you willing to be?

To whom in your group would it be best for you to be accountable?

Now make sure that everyone in the group has an "Accountability Partner" with whom he or she will be share struggles and victories.

CHAPTER FOURTEEN

WORKING EXPECTANTLY

Disciple Quality: **ALERTNESS**

WHAT IT SAYS

LESSON FORTY
Read Luke 21:5-36

The people of God have always been fascinated with the future, and rightly so, because we know history is going somewhere. The prophets frequently spoke and wrote about *The Day of the Lord*, referring to the consummation of the ages when God would interrupt human history on earth and bring about his kingdom. It was not at all unusual or unexpected that the followers of Jesus would wonder how their Messiah would fulfill the eschatological hopes of the Jewish people.

This passage, Luke 21:5-36 is known as the Lord's Apocalyptic Discourse. It is essentially the same teaching found in Matthew 24 and Mark 13. The word *apocalyptic* comes from the Greek word meaning "revelation," and in fact, the Greek name of the last book of the Bible is *Apocalypsis*.

From 200 B.C. to 200 A.D. apocalyptic writing was quite popular. Briefly, apocalyptic literature is characterized by: 1) the attempt to predict the future, 2) use of mysterious imagery, 3) allusion to cosmic warfare, and 4) a high degree of drama. This type of writing was used for various reasons. Like modern mysteries, apocalyptic literature bordered on the sensational, which readers always find appealing. Sometimes writers used this genre to give greater credence or authority to their message. Occasionally, apocalyptic writing contained a coded message, which the author wanted only a select group to understand.

This later purpose may have been part of John's motive in writing Revelation. There are many references in Revelation to events and people contemporary to the writing. As persecution of Christians was beginning to intensify, John's message of hope, his vision of the glorified Christ, and his many veiled allusions to the Roman Empire were well understood by first and second century Christians, but not by outsiders to the faith.

> *Jesus told his followers, in a manner of speaking, that it was none of their business when the end would come.*

The Apocalypse of Jesus is much shorter and more focused in purpose than John's Revelation. Jesus gave the teaching in response to questions by the disciples after Jesus predicted the destruction of the temple. Convinced that Jesus was the Messiah, the disciples anticipated the soon coming of the Day of the Lord, and hearing that the temple would be destroyed, they naturally assumed that would signal the end. Without answering their questions specifically, he used the occasion to teach them **alertness.**

1. The questions the disciples asked in verse 7 are similarly posed in Mark 13:4 and Matthew 24:3. How many questions did they actually ask him?

    What assumption were they making?

    Why did Jesus not correct their mistaken assumption?

2. Notice the events Jesus described in verses 8-11. These are often thought to be signs of the end. What did Jesus say about these events?

3. Verses 25-28 refer to Old Testament imagery about the Day of the Lord. What similarities do you see in:

    Isaiah 13:9-10

    Joel 2:10-11

    Zephaniah 1:14-15

    Daniel 7:13-14

    These signs have not yet occurred. What must happen before these signs? See Matthew 24:14.

    What does this suggest to us about **alertness**?

4. What do verses 34-36 say to disciples about **alertness**?

    What kinds of things threaten our **alertness**?

    More specifically, what threatens your **alertness**?

    Parallel verses are Mark 13:33-37. What do these verses add to the warning?

5. Matthew's account uses a parable in 21:45-51. What is the main force of this parable?

    What is the relationship between **alertness** and stewardship?

WHAT IT MEANS

LESSON FORTY-ONE

Nearly two thousand years have passed since the Lord gave the Apocalyptic Discourse, and Christians still await his return. Obviously, the destruction of the temple in 70 A.D. had very little to do with the end times. Much of the Lord's Apocalyptic Discourse, however, referred to first century events, not the end times. Fortunately, the early disciples remembered his prophecy, and they fled from Jerusalem when the Romans invaded. Most Jews did not flee, and thousands of them were slaughtered. No doubt those fleeing disciples thought they were seeing the beginning of the end. The end time (*eschaton* in Greek) technically refers to all that time from the first coming of Jesus to his future coming as King. We have been in the last days ever since Jesus came. His delay in returning has convinced many to stop expecting him. Various imaginative theories have been put forward to explain that Jesus must not have meant that he personally would come to earth.

Such skepticism is not new. Already in Peter's day, some were asking with a doubtful voice where Jesus was. Peter reminded his readers that God does not operate within our time frame. His plans for history may not be according to our wishes (2 Peter 3:3-9). Jesus himself does not know the precise time of his return, according to Matthew 24:36. His greater concern is the readiness of his people when he does return (Luke 18:8).

> *We have been in the last days ever since Jesus came.*

6. In the early part of his discourse what kind of alertness did Jesus command?

    How can we be alert in this way?

7. Verses 12-24 seem to be addressed to the immediate disciples (notice how many times Jesus used the personal pronouns *you* and *your*). What principles here might apply to all disciples?

8. Within just a few days of hearing the Lord's admonition, the **alertness** of the disciples would be tested. How did they succeed or fail each of these tests?

    Luke 22:7-13

    Luke 22:20-23

    Luke 22:39-46

    Luke 22:54-62

9. Notice how Jesus responded to the question the disciples asked him in verse 7. What does that suggest about how we should approach the study of the end times?

10. The events in verses 20-24 occurred in 70 A.D. Is it likely that verses will be fulfilled again?

    If so, what does this say to us about **alertness**?

    If not, what does this say to us about **alertness**?

11. What do Mark 13:34 and 36 say about how we should be alert?

    Why is **alertness** an important leadership quality?

WHAT IT MEANS FOR ME

LESSON FORTY-TWO

Jesus' purpose in giving the teaching was not to satisfy the curiosity of the disciples, but to warn them and instill in them the quality of **alertness.** Nevertheless, their curiosity was not checked. A few months later—after his resurrection—the disciples asked Jesus whether now was the time he would overthrow the Romans and restore the kingdom to Israel (Acts 1:6). The reply of Jesus should be a rebuke to modern prophecy enthusiasts, especially those who think that studying prophecy is truly getting into the meat of the Word. (Hebrews 5:12 and 6:1-2 ought to confirm that speculation about the end times is spiritual milk, at best.) Jesus told his followers, in a manner of speaking, that it was none of their business when the end would come. Their task was to bear witness to him to the most remote parts of the earth.

Although thinking about the end times is stimulating, that is not the theme of this unit of lessons. Our focus is on the character quality of **alertness**. By this we mean not the crystal ball gazing kind of **alertness**, trying to calculate the time of Jesus' return, but the kind of **alertness** that preoccupies us with being busily ready. The warning of Jesus to be watchful does not tell us to wait passively; rather, he warned his people to make sure we are expecting him at all times and never to let down our spiritual guard. The best way to watch is to be serving, which is why this chapter is entitled *Working Expectantly*.

12. In what circumstances are you particularly aware of your surroundings and especially alert? Think of several situations and describe each briefly.

    In each of those situations what did **alertness** actually mean? How did it affect you mentally, emotionally and physically?

    Would you say that in each of those situations that you chose to be alert, or was **alertness** somehow thrust upon you by the nature of the situation?

13. What events might people of our day assume would be the sign of the end?

14. Do you think it is wrong or dangerous to become fascinated about the end times? Why or why not?

15. Based on all the observations you have made about **alertness** in these three lessons, what would you consider to be the opposite of **alertness**? How can you avoid that?

16. What changes have been made in your perspective on prophecy and the end times by studying these scriptures?

17. Putting all your obligations, priorities, and needs in perspectives, what two or three things should you do to grow in the quality of **alertness**?

Pray for each other to grow in the area of **alertness**.

NOW WHAT?

Kingdom Strategy #14

Every day is lived and worked with a sense of anticipation and alertness by disciples because they expect that their Lord may return at any moment.

What does it mean for modern disciples to be watchful and alert? Simply to sit on the sidelines, ready for anything? No, it certainly does not mean that we should be idle or passive. Paul severely admonished the Thessalonians about this. Apparently some were convinced that Jesus would return very soon, so they stopped working. The apostle warned them that they must follow his example and continue their labors so they *"would not be a burden"* to anyone (2 Thessalonians 3:7-8).

Jesus himself told us how he expects his people to be watchful. *"Who then is the faithful and wise servant, whom the master has put in charge of the servants in his household to give them their food at the proper time? It will be good for that servant whose master finds him doing so when he returns"* (Matt. 24:45-46). In Mark's Gospel, Jesus expands on the concept by suggesting that one of the servants would be assigned to keep watch at the door: *". . .because you do not know when the owner of the house will come back. . . . If he comes suddenly, don't let him find you sleeping. What I say to you, I say to everyone: `Watch!'"* (Mark 13:35-37).

Just what is it, then, that he wants us to be doing in our **alertness**? Jesus wants us to be *working*—to be making disciples by witnessing in his name.

Matthew 25 follows the Apocalyptic Discourse in that Gospel, and consists of three lengthy parables that address three aspects of **alertness**. Divide your group in three, and ask each group to study one of these parables:

- The parable of the ten virgins: Matthew 25:1-13
- The parable of the talents: Matthew 25:14-30
- The parable of the sheep and goats: Matthew 25:31-46

a. Discuss what each parable adds to your understanding of **alertness.**

b. What negative and positive examples are found in each parable?

c. What have the positive characters done differently than the negative ones?

d. What rationalizations did the negative characters use to excuse their failure?

e. Which of the three parables speaks most poignantly to you?

f. What do you need to do be more alert?

CHAPTER FIFTEEN

ACHIEVING GREATNESS

Disciple Quality: **SERVANTHOOD**

WHAT IT SAYS

LESSON FORTY-THREE
Read Luke 22:24-30

One of the Church's most prominent practices is the communion service, known also as the Lord's Supper or the Eucharist. People who know little else about our faith often know we practice this rather bazaar ceremony which symbolizes drinking blood. Even in the first century, Christians were wrongly accused of being cannibalistic. Suspicious pagans spread the rumor that the "love feasts" of the Christians were drunken orgies which resulted in sacrificing a child and eating its flesh and drinking its blood as an act of worship to Christ.

That wrong outlook on the Lord's Supper was horrendous, but at least it took the meal seriously. In today's text, the disciples seemed to have missed completely the solemnness and sacredness of the event. Before the last sips of the sacred wine had been swallowed, the disciples were arguing about which of them was thought to be the greatest.

> *The disciples seemed to have missed completely the solemnness and sacredness of the event.*

Aren't you glad the Gospel writers were so honest! The men who would soon become leaders in the early church are here presented as self-centered, insensitive, normal people. In history's most heavenly moment, an event demystifying and giving finality to religion's most significant ceremony, the Feast of Passover, and at the same time foreshadowing the great messianic banquet yet to come, the key participants were totally self-absorbed. If they were not able to hallow the moment in intimacy with Jesus, at least they might have put on a religious face as other self-respecting Jews would do at the Passover.

Despite their lack of reverence for the meal and their lack of sensitivity to his comment about being betrayed, Jesus did not use the occasion to chastise his disciples. Rather, he seized the opportunity to teach them about kingdom greatness. Their time for sitting at a table and being served, and even holding authority over the twelve tribes of Israel, would come (Luke 22:30). Until then, the lowly path of **servanthood**, similar to the example of Jesus, would be expected of them.

1. What do you think prompted the disciples' dispute at the communion table about which of them was considered to be greatest?

2. How might they have understood the statements Jesus made about his body and his blood (vv.18-20)?

3. How might Jesus' remarks to Peter in verses 31 and 32 relate to the issue of leadership and greatness?

4. Peter surely was the leader of the apostles, yet he seemed to err more often than the others. What does this suggest about leadership?

    How can we discover potential leaders?

    How can we help them achieve their potential?

5. Did the apostles violate **servanthood** leadership in Acts 6:1-4? If not, what other principle is at work here?

WHAT IT MEANS

LESSON FORTY-FOUR

At issue in this corrected understanding of greatness is a person's appraisal of worth. Our world teaches that our value lies in proportion to our power, i.e., how many people or resources we can control. Greatness seems to have little to do with character and everything to do with power. Overpowering others with our authority, whether by position or personality, is seen to be a mark of positive achievement. Coach Vince Lombardi of the Green Bay Packers used to say, "Winning isn't everything; it's the only thing." That mentality may be alright on the football field (but then again, maybe it isn't), but it certainly is not a Christian concept.

The disciples got into trouble in this passage because they were too fond of winning. Verse 24 says a dispute arose among them; the Greek word for dispute is *philoneikia*, meaning love of victory. People often use relationships to enhance their sense of self-worth by viewing encounters as win/lose opportunities. A large body of literature is devoted to training people to be winners, the assumption always being that victories are more important than relationships. And winning means getting others to serve you.

Quite contrary to that view is Jesus' definition of true greatness. Empowering others by serving them is greater than overpowering them. Being on their side to help them win is better than competing with them to help yourself win. Greatness in the kingdom is more important than greatness in the boardroom.

Authority is not to be lorded over others but to lift others. Serving at the table is more Christ-like than sitting at the table.

These lessons are hard to learn, not hard to understand, but hard to learn. Human nature and society's values entice us to use power for selfish advantage and excuse it by calling it leadership or looking out for number one, or some such expression.

> *Empowering others by serving them is greater than overpowering them.*

6. What are some of the characteristics of "Gentile" style leadership (v.25) that you observe in your circles?

    Do you think the **servanthood** style that Jesus taught would work in today's corporate environment? Do you know of examples?

    Is the **servanthood** style of leadership primarily for church workers, or is it applicable to all situations?

7. What results can be expected from the "Gentile" style leadership?

    What results can be expected from **servanthood** leadership?

    Why is **servanthood** a key quality for kingdom leaders?

8. Should Christians seek to have power? Authority?

    If so, how can they ensure that they use it appropriately?

    If not, what should be our outlook on leadership in the world?

9. How can leaders equip others to serve and delegate responsibility to them, while at the same time be the ones who serve at the tables themselves? See verse 27.

10. How did Jesus illustrate at this meal his teaching about greatness and leadership?

WHAT IT MEANS FOR ME

LESSON FORTY-FIVE

As you work through this last lesson, be honest with one another about motives. Most church people serve in some capacity, but if we understand Jesus rightly, true greatness lies in serving humbly, not caring about being the greatest, but about being useful.

Some people have learned the subtle art of passive aggression by which they manipulate others with a feigned subservience. They serve, but with a hidden and selfish agenda. While we must be careful not to judge others' motives, we must also be alert to this possibility. In religious settings especially, this is a problem. Spiritually minded people respect a servant spirit so much that sometimes a person is received into leadership simply because he appears to live to please others, while all the time his only concern is to use them as stepping stones to greater heights. Such a person is the ultimate political animal. He knows he will thrive very well in the atmosphere of the church if he learns to play the game well enough.

> *The mark of true greatness is being content with never receiving credit for one's work.*

Discerning the integrity of one who appears to have a servant's heart may usually be done easily. The mark of true greatness is being content with never receiving credit for one's work. Those who happily serve provided they are appropriately rewarded with human applause or appreciation do not merit Christ's commendation of greatness.

11. In what areas of your life are you expected to be a leader?

    How would you assess your effectiveness as a server in each area, and what style have you been using?

    What changes, if any, do you need to make to become a more effective leader?

12. In what areas of your life is love of winning sometimes a problem?

    How can love of winning be converted into a positive motive in relationships?

    Talk with others in your group about how you might use your influence more to build up others than to win.

13. In what area(s) of your life would you like to be great?

    Is it realistic to think you will achieve greatness in that area? If so, what do you need to do to get there?

14. Having come to the end of this discipleship course, are you ready to disciple others?

    If not, what are you lacking?

    How might this principle of **servanthood** leadership enable you to do what you think you cannot do?

    If you are ready to disciple others, who will you recruit, and when will you ask them?

15. As a discipleship group, pray for guidance about your next steps as you respond to the Master who continues to say "Follow Me."

    Pray for each other to grow in the area of **servanthood.**

NOW WHAT?

Kingdom Strategy #15

Leadership in the kingdom of God is not attained through professional status, economic success, or natural ability, but through the humble, selfless spirit of servanthood.

Serving others is not to be viewed as a stepping-stone to greater power and position. Jesus was not saying that if his followers wished to rise to great heights in the church, they must first prove themselves in a lowly place. Not at all. That principle is used effectively in the world, but it reflects an improper attitude because it caters to selfish ambition. Jesus was saying that faithful service in a lowly place is itself true greatness. Stepping-stone service is out of step with our Lord. Likewise, if we refuse to allow others to serve us, it is likely that we are rendering our service with a wrong motivation. Kingdom living requires that service be rendered and accepted with a noncompetitive spirit. Self-advancement must never be its goal

Think of Peter's response to the foot-washing incident: *"Lord, are you going to wash my feet?..No, you shall never wash my feet"* (John 13:6, 8). This falls into the category of prideful one-upmanship. Humility is a necessary element of spiritual leadership, and receiving someone else's service can be more humbling than rendering service ourselves. Whether serving or being served, our motive should never be "What's in it for me?" True **servanthood** is an act of love, totally devoid of selfish striving toward personal goals. We are to allow that love to flow freely in either direction.

"Corporate culture is an important idea in the modern business world. Managers who want to create the best environment for work have learned the principle that people are more important than products, projects, and even profit. Achieving the corporate culture of the kingdom of God is even more demanding of its leaders. Because the goals of the kingdom are eternal and so very special, greatness of leadership cannot be judged by the world's standards, which brings us to Kingdom Strategy # 15—which may be the most important one of all.

It's time now for some evaluation of your discipleship growth. On the next page indicate your growth since you began this discipleship study by putting a check at the appropriate place on the line of each character quality. After each person in the group has had a chance to complete the assessment, share your findings. Obviously, the qualities that you have checked closest to the left represent the cutting edge for further spiritual growth for you. Ask one of the people in your group who is strong in that quality to help you achieve that growth. Be open (teachable) to the impressions that others have of your growth, and discuss how as a group you might be able to continue to encourage one another into deeper discipleship.

Where you have checked qualities close to the right are areas of strength for you, and provide good opportunities and responsibilities to use those qualities in ministry. Ask God to use your discipleship in those areas to make disciples of others.

APPENDIX

ASSESSING YOUR PROGRESS IN THE 15 DISCIPLESHIP QUALITIES

Low	Quality	High
know it all, authoritarian, domineering, arrogant	Teachability (Luke 5:1-11)	willing to heed other's ideas or directions; a listener
Proper, orthodox, precise, meticulous, rigid, unbending	Flexibility (Luke 5:27-39)	willing to take risks, let go of established ways
concerned with title, image; seeks to be center of attention	Humility (Luke 6:20-26)	not thinking of self, personal image; identify with the lowly
retaliates against those who slight or hurt; seeks revenge	Compassion (Luke 6:27-38)	reconciler; shows kindness and mercy, love, even to an enemy
blind to own inconsistency; mixed motives; deceitful	Integrity (Luke 6:37-49)	consistent, adheres to same standards in all situations; truthful
"looking out for number one"	Selflessness (Luke 9:18-27)	without concern for own comfort, well being or pleasure
easily distracted by, and wastes time on, the unimportant	Intensity (Luke 9:57-62)	keeps commitment to serve God and neighbor first at all times
"goes with the flow"; avoids involvement; follows majority	Courage (Luke 10:1-24)	gets involved with hurting people; stands against popular opinion
"the rugged individualist," self-made; no need for God or others	Dependency (Luke 11:1-13)	places full trust and confidence in God, depending on him for all
puts a "positive spin" on things, preferring to appear better than reality	Transparency (Luke 12:1-12)	reveals truth even if costly

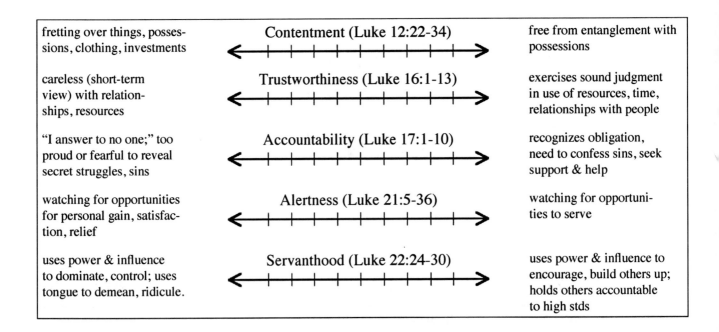

Last assignment. Would you please send to MasterWorks an assessment of this material? Be as specific or general as you want. We need to be held accountable by you! Thank you.

MasterWorks, Inc.
David E. Schroeder, Founder
info@masterworksinc.org

---

[i] Ralph Neighbour. *The Seven Last Words of the Church*. Grand Rapids, MI: Zondervan, 1973.

[ii] Francis Frangipane. *Holiness, Truth and the Presence of God*. Cedar Rapids, IA: Arrow Publications, 1986.

[iii] Andrew Murray. *Humility*. Ada, MI: Baker Publishing Group, 2001.

[iv] Henri Nouwen. *Reaching Out*. Glasgow: William Collins, 1976.

[v] Norval Geldenhuys. *Commentary on the Gospel of Luke*. Grand Rapids, MI: Eerdmans, 1975.

[vi] William Barclay. *The Gospel of Luke*. Westminster: John Knox Press, 2001.

[vii] *Book of Common Prayer of the Reformed Episcopal Church*. Philadelphia, PA: Reformed Episcopal Publication Society, p. 6, 1889.

[viii] Ibid.

[ix] Dietrich Bonhoeffer. *The Cost of Discipleship*. New York, NY: SCM Publishing Ltd, 1959.

[x] Howard Hendricks. *Herald of Holiness*, Vol. 84. Madison, WI: Nazarene Publishing House, 1995.

[xi] Richard Foster. *Money, Sex, & Power*. San Francisco, CA: Harper & Row, 1985

CPSIA information can be obtained
at www.ICGtesting.com
Printed in the USA
FFOW05n1500120317

9 781628 394559